Beyond
Note
Cards

Beyond Note cards

Rethinking the Freshman Research Paper

Bruce Ballenger

Boynton/Cook Publishers
HEINEMANN
Portsmouth, NH

For Donald Murray.

In his shadow I have walked with words.

Boynton/Cook Publishers, Inc.
A subsidiary of Reed Elsevier Inc.
361 Hanover Street
Portsmouth, NH 03801–3912
http://www.boyntoncook.com

Offices and agents throughout the world

Library of Congress Cataloging-in-Publication Data
Ballenger, Bruce P.
     Beyond note cards: rethinking the freshman research paper/Bruce Ballenger.
          p.   cm.
     Includes bibliographical references.
     ISBN 0-86709-479-6
     1. Report writing—Study and teaching (Higher)—United States.
     2. Research—Study and teaching (Higher)—United States.
     3. Academic writing—Study and teaching (Higher)—United States.
     4. English language—Rhetoric—Study and teaching—United States.
     I. Title
     LB2369.B244   1999   98-48823
     378.1'70281—dc21   CIP

Editor: William Varner
Production: Elizabeth Valway
Cover design: Joni Doherty Design
Manufacturing: Louise Richardson

Printed in the United States of America on acid-free paper
03 02 01 00 99 DA 1 2 3 4 5

Contents

Acknowledgments

Fifteen years ago, fresh from a stint in Montana, I became a graduate student at the University of New Hampshire. I was awarded a teaching assistantship, and for the first time was charged with teaching undergraduates how to write a research paper. I imagined that I would do it fairly well—I had some teaching experience and I had done some research, and I had certainly written lots of term papers. But I was wrong. My students and I hated the research assignment, though we all dutifully slogged through it. Not long after I started teaching at UNH, Thomas Newkirk took over as director of the freshman writing program, succeeding Gary Lindbergh, a fine and gentle man who first inspired me to teach composition. Sadly, Gary passed away a few years later. Tom Newkirk knew of my frustration with the research paper, and urged me to try some different approaches. As an incentive, he told me I would present to the writing faculty on the topic at one of our weekly meetings. It was a shrewd move. Somehow I would have to come up with something new to say. Tom invited me to address faculty meetings on teaching the research paper every year he was writing director, and suddenly I had a speciality. Years later, when Tom directed my dissertation committee, I began writing this book. I doubt very much if I would have found my own way to this rich and complicated topic if it hadn't been for Tom's encouragement and his faith that I had something useful to say about it. Tom Newkirk taught me a lot of things, and one of them was how to be a mentor who knows how to combine faith, guidance, and encouragement into an intellectually combustible mixture. The flame has been burning ever since.

There are other important characters in this narrative, too. One is Lad Tobin. I know Lad as an important composition scholar, but also as a teammate on the 1967 cross country team at Highland Park High School. We rediscovered each other a few years ago as new PhD's in the same field, and from the beginning Lad encouraged me to pursue this topic. His questions and published work have deepened my own thinking. Brock Dethier, now at Utah State, is another close friend and collaborator who has seen me through the many evolutions of this project. He taught me to think on my ice skates. Melody Graulich, Robert Connors, Patricia Sullivan, and Jeff Bolster all contributed directly to strengthening this manuscript. Melody helped me to see the literary connections and how to make my prose more graceful, Bob was invaluable on the historical narrative, Pat asked wonderful questions that refocused my thinking and reminded me what I didn't know I knew, and Jeff offered a useful perspective as one in another discipline. I'm deeply grateful to them all.

Among the others who contributed to this work, I'd like to thank Barry Lane—another old friend and co-author—who has been beating the drum for change in research paper pedagogy for as long as I have, but who graciously gives me credit for making the most noise. There were many voices in my head as I wrote, and they included Cheryl Johnson, Michelle Payne, Victor Villanueva, Anne Maxim-Kastrinos, Rachel Edelson, Don Jones, Greg Bowe, Carol Kountz, Tony Nevin, and Leaf Seligman.

I'm extremely grateful to the two students featured in this book—Carrie Hill and Michael Davis—both of whom generously contributed their time and papers and patience. Rebecca Hodgkins graciously contributed her high school research materials and her thoughts about them. Jayne Wynters was the student who first triggered my thinking about the research paper. Since then, I've had hundreds of students at UNH and Boise State University who have helped me develop these ideas.

Thanks as well to Heinemann and Boynton/Cook—the leading publisher of books for writing teachers—and especially to Bill Varner, the editor in charge of this project. From the beginning, Bill was everything a writer hopes an editor will be: flexible, considerate, generous with criticism and praise, and smart.

Finally, I reserve my deepest gratitude for my family, especially my wife Karen, who has seen me through enough of these projects to know when I need an ear or a gentle push, or when I need to be left alone. How fortunate that over twenty years ago the office photocopier jammed and flashed "call key operator." We've been humming along ever since.

Introduction

Huck, Tom, and the Pleaders for Euthanasia

In the early chapters of Mark Twain's *Adventures of Huckleberry Finn*, Huck is enlisted by Tom Sawyer to join his gang, a band to which all the boys pledge loyalty, taking a blood oath and swearing to secrecy. "What's the line of business of this Gang?" asks one of the boys. "Nothing, only robbery and murder," Tom said.

> "But who are we going to rob? houses—or cattle—or—"
>
> "Stuff! stealing cattle and such things ain't robbery, it's burglary," says Tom Sawyer. "We ain't burglars. That ain't no sort of style. We are highwaymen. We stop stages and carriages on the road, with masks on, and kill the people and take their watches and money."
>
> "Must we always kill the people?"
>
> "Oh, certainly. It's best. Some authorities think different, but mostly it's considered best to kill them. Except some that you bring to the cave here and keep them till they're ransomed."
>
> "Ransomed? What's that?"
>
> "I don't know. But that's what they do. I've seen it in books; and so of course that's what we've got to do."
>
> "But how can we do it if we don't know what it is?"
>
> "Why blame it all, we've *got* to do it. Don't I tell you it's in the books? Do you want to go to doing different from what's in the books, and get things all muddled up?" (32)

Armed with "lathe and broomsticks" (34), the Tom Sawyer Gang never does ransom anyone, much less murder them, and the closest the band comes to accosting a carriage is overturning a turnip cart. The

1

scheme is typically Sawyerian—all style and no substance—but Huck persists in playing along, at least for a while. He and the other boys yield willingly to Tom's authority, an authority derived in large part from his ability to recite the narrative elements of Romantic novels he doesn't really understand. But Tom's power comes from a particular kind of epistemology. The "regular way" to do something, according to Tom Sawyer, is not based on information gleaned from direct experience, or on testing textual claims against observed reality. Things must simply go by the book—an often awkward, and frequently silly, imitation of someone else's story of what is or what should be. Tom is never an author of his own experience; instead, he is authored.

This doesn't make much sense to Huck—which in Tom's view makes his friend a "perfect sap-head" (36)—but he submits to Tom's schemes until it becomes clear to Huck that he has nothing to learn from them. For at the heart of Huck's compliance, as Michael Bell argues, is *curiosity* (55).

"I wanted to see the camels and elephants," says Huck, who reluctantly agrees to join Tom and the gang in an ambush on a "parcel of Spanish merchants and rich A-rabs" who were supposedly camping nearby. When it turns out to be a Sunday school picnic, Tom claims that Huck simply can't see the "A-rabs" and their elephants because magic turned them into an "infant Sunday school." Huck finally quits the gang in disgust—"we hadn't killed any people, but only pretended" (34). But he never loses the curiosity that drives him through his world, attending to particulars of sunrise on the river, exploring a dangerous steamboat wreck, or studying the melancholy poetry and morose crayon drawings of Emmeline Grangerford. Huck's adventures, unlike Tom's, are never mediated by other texts, nor does he share Tom's concern for convention. Huck is always willing to entertain authoritative claims—that he would get whatever he asked for through prayer, that the movement of chickens means rain, or that there really *were* two hundred elephants and six hundred camels as Tom claimed—but he always viewed them as testable claims, revised or rejected based on his own direct experience. *The Adventures of Huckleberry Finn* reports the results of his research.

For many years, as a teacher of college composition, I have been guilty of turning Hucks into Toms. I remember the moment I first realized this. In the summer of 1984, I was teaching a section of Freshman English to a group of mostly enthusiastic students at the University of New Hampshire. Things were progressing nicely, I thought; a number of students were writing compelling and sometimes insightful essays, including a young woman named Jayne, who wrote a piece titled "The Sterile Cage," which I photocopied for the entire class. I still do. The essay was a moving account of Jayne's struggle with a bone disorder, and the time she spent as a child in a hospital, suspended in a stainless steel frame that kept her immobile. The writing was moving her—and her readers—towards a fresh understanding of that part of her life, and at times the prose shimmered.

Unfortunately (or so I thought at the time), the course was also moving, away from essays and towards the required research paper assignment. I shared with my colleagues the widespread dread and dissatisfaction with this assignment, and the sense that it was a necessary evil. I disliked how cold the classroom became when the subject of the research paper came up—the sometimes surly silences and sighs—and quickly longed to return to teaching the essay, something for which my students developed some genuine enthusiasm. But I also shared the vague belief that the assignment had "practical" value, that I was teaching students valuable things about using the library, avoiding plagiarism, and modeling academic writing. I was also certain that, at least in this class, I had prepared some students to write with more confidence and authority, and that it would carry over into the extended, source-based writing they were about to tackle. Jayne would write a good research paper, I thought, because she's such a good writer.

She chose a topic in childhood development—something I see now was directly related to her exploration in "The Sterile Cage"—and though she said the research was going well, I could tell it was loveless labor for her. When I finally came across Jayne's paper in the stack of drafts one evening, I eagerly began to read it. It was bad. Though she obviously researched the subject vigorously, demonstrating an impressive bibliography, Jayne's paper was unfocused, her analysis lifeless, the prose wooden. The voice she had found in her essays was missing, as was her usual talent for getting to the heart of a topic. I distinctly remember the conference we had in my office a week later because it was so unpleasant.

What did she think of the paper? I asked. "Not much."

Did she find it unfocused? "Sort of."

Did the paper sound lifeless to her? "Yes."

Jayne glared across the desk at me.

"What do you want from me?" she said. "This is a research paper, goddammit. It's *supposed* to be this way."

Something is wrong with an assignment, I reflected later, that turns a good writer into a bad one. A few weeks earlier Jayne had been writing with purpose and authority, and even grace. I sensed that she had permanently altered her relationship to language, and that at least in her essay writing she had struggled successfully for the ownership of words. Jayne had clearly lost that struggle in her research paper, creating an alien discourse that we both recognized belonged entirely to someone else. Her paper was an empty, lifeless, and ritualistic performance, mimicking what she believed were the conventions of the research paper genre. I picked up Jayne's draft expecting Huckleberry Finn but got Tom Sawyer instead, and I wondered what had gone wrong.

Unfortunately, it took the failure of one of my better writing students with the research paper to stun me into a reexamination of the assignment, despite witnessing similar struggles by less gifted writers through the years. With few exceptions the research papers I received from most students in Freshman English were disappointing. I think I had grown accustomed to disappointment, an attitude that has hovered over this assignment ever since it made its first appearance as a recognized genre in college composition texts in the 1930s and 1940s. In fact, the research paper—or "source theme," "investigatory paper," "library paper," or "term paper," as it has been variously described through the years—has generated a legacy of complaint among composition instructors and their students that is probably unmatched by any other single writing assignment. "Among the most ardent pleaders for euthanasia," wrote W.L.T. Fleischaur in a 1941 *College English* article, "is the instructor of freshman composition in those colleges where the teaching of the investigatory paper is required" (75). Another writer in the same journal thirteen years later called the typical research paper assignment the "one-great-chore which exhausts freshman and instructor more surely than it exhausts the library's resources on the volcanoes of Hawaii or Swedish holiday cookery" (Eldredge 228). Everett W. Gibbs, in an acerbic 1960 article in *College Composition and Communication*, titled "Freshman Research Papers—Once More," called them "a mockery of intellectual activity" (82). And Janet Kotler, giving a more contemporary, but familiar, negative spin on the research paper in *Freshman English News* began a 1989 article this way:

> Let's talk about the research paper—granted, a dispiriting proposal. But although it bores everybody damn near to death, a great many college courses, certainly every composition class, have A RE-SEARCH PAPER (business communications texts, depressingly, often call it THE LONG REPORT) embedded in them like a stone.
>   And we all hate it. (33)

Writing instructors, however, would be hard-pressed to work up the venom many students summon when reflecting on their experiences writing research papers. "It involved going to the library after school for about two hours, reading things by other people and then making note cards," said Pat, reflecting on her high school papers. "Next came an outline, then a final draft, each year for four years. . . . The teachers would always be angry at me because, and I quote, I 'thought too much while writing the paper.' What did a teacher mean by thinking too much?" Another student added, "The definition of research is tiresome studies on a subject that a person does not like."

Sometimes, apparently, student dislike of the research paper even deepens into psychological trauma. Robert Esch, in an amusing—and disturbing—1975 article in *College Composition and Communication*, gives an account of a student who approached him a few days before the deadline for the final draft of the research paper. "Mr. Esch, I had a dream about you last night," she said. She then described a dream in which Esch pushed a button for a trap door, through which the student fell into a basement room where he had trapped other university students, all of whom were working on research papers surrounded by "stacks of 3×5 and 5×7 note cards . . . and all types of colored binders for themes" (43).

> "All of those people were trying to write the *perfect* research paper. Some of them I recognized. Others had been down there in that room for over 20 years, and no one had heard from them.
> "And do you know what you did when they finally turned in a paper that you found acceptable?"
> "God knows, what?"
> "You stood them up against the wall and shot them" (43).

Though they rarely report dream disturbances, student complaints about the research paper are widespread. They are also not a new phenomenon. When two researchers in 1931 surveyed the students and teachers at Kansas State Teachers College about their attitudes towards the college "term paper," 67% of the students agreed that the benefit of the assignment did not exceed the time and energy it required (Brown and Baldwin 311). Fifty-three percent supported the abolishment of *all* term papers altogether (312). Ten years later, a survey of Queens College faculty and students on the term paper assignment reported student dissatisfaction with papers on assigned topics, "which destroyed enthusiasm for the work" and the fact that papers seldom seem to be "written as the instructors intend them to be" (Rivlin 317). Students also "condemned the ridiculous attempt at being original when they knew so little about the subject that they were not entitled to an original opinion" (318). To be sure, there are some students who have had positive experiences with research papers. Some cite the usefulness of learning "library procedures," while others recall papers from which they learned a great deal, but when prompted to talk about it, these students almost invariably point out the ways in which their successful assignments strayed from what they viewed as the traditional research paper.

So widespread, apparently, is the "research paper blues" among college students that in the last twenty years an industry has grown in sales of prewritten research reports. Research Assistance, one of the largest of these retailers, claims that it offers more than twenty thousand research reports, each written by "talented writers" who are "expert in their various areas of expertise." In an interesting bit of self-justification, Dr. Cynthia Stone, "Research Director" of Research Associates, writes prospective clients that "solid research ability is one of the most important ingredients of success in college today." Sadly, she notes, "one of the major reasons that otherwise excellent students do poorly in research and writing aspects of their courses is that they are just not well prepared by their high school experience." Why, Dr. Stone asks, should these "otherwise excellent students" be penalized for the faulty pedagogy of their high school teachers and "receive lower grades than they're entitled to?" No reason whatsoever, as long as Research Associates is around. For $7.50 a page, the company will send a photocopy of a term paper on one of the twenty thousand topics listed in its annual catalogue, or it will custom write a paper on short notice. The range of rates for a custom undergraduate paper is $20 to $25 per page, while graduate students pay twice that.

The mail-order term paper business, however, has been eclipsed by Web sites on the Internet that boast of large inventories of "ready-made" or special order research papers. (For more on student research and the Internet, see Appendix C.) At last count, there were at least 40 such sites on the Internet. While most of them claim that the papers they make available are to be used as "study aids" or serve as "models," a number of online term paper companies offer overnight service for a hefty fee. For example, the New Jersey–based "Paper Store" ("Term Papers Got 'Ya Diggin' Yourself Into A Grave?") offers "exclusive emergency service" for students who presumably need a "model" the morning their paper is due. For $18.95 a page, plus an $18.95-per-page surcharge, the company's team of writers (all of whom have "no less than Master's degrees in their respective fields" and have completed the company's "exclusive research and writing training course") will deliver a custom-written paper on any topic by "sunrise the next morning." Several of these sites, the most notorious of which is called "SchoolSucks.Com," allow students to download term papers for free.[1]

Perusing the inventory of archived term papers, it's not hard to see which are some of the more popular topics for undergraduate researchers. For example, Research Assistance's catalogue lists eleven papers on steroid use by athletes, and eleven on Melville's *Moby Dick*. The abortion topic features more than forty papers. Just pick a side of the debate and there's a paper for you:

> 17760-Pro-Choice Position on Abortion. Personal freedom, self determination, *Roe v. Wade*, public good, role of government. Counters anti-abortion view. (12 footnotes, 7 bibliographic citations, 6 pages).

with source-based writing, and why have our pedagogies failed to produce satisfactory papers? Why do we teach the research paper in the first place? What are its aims? Is there any evidence that this assignment can do what we hope it will do?

Remarkably, composition scholars over the years have largely begged—or ignored—those questions. Compilers of a bibliography of over two hundred articles published between 1923 and 1980 on teaching the research paper noted that while the vast majority are exclusively devoted to pedagogy, "few are theoretical in nature or based on research, and almost none cites even one other work on the subject." The authors add, "There are no real experts on all aspects of the research paper" (Ford, Rees, and Ward 84). My own survey of the literature since 1980 suggests that the dearth of theory on the assignment is a condition that has changed only slightly. While there are now a handful of theorists who are writing about the research paper (Brent; Larson; Schwegler and Shamoon; Ford; Wilson; Nelson), most published articles on the topic (when they appear, which isn't often) offer ideas only about pedagogy. In *Reading as Rhetorical Invention*, Douglas Brent observes that there is nothing especially faulty with the mass of articles on research paper pedagogy, but that composition theory has simply lagged behind.

> Composition teachers . . . do not have an encompassing definition
> of what it really means to compose discourse based on other
> people's texts. What does it really mean to search, not just through
> one's own storehouse of knowledge and values, but through other
> writers' storehouses, in search of the answer to a question? What
> does it mean to interpret large numbers of often-conflicting texts,
> evaluate the opinions expressed, and create from an amalgam of
> one's own and other people's beliefs a new answer, a new piece of
> knowledge that is not just a patchwork of sources but an original
> system of beliefs that could not have existed without the believer's
> having considered other texts? (103)

It's my purpose here to both theorize about the aims of research paper instruction and student difficulties with source-based writing as well as propose a pedagogy that grows out of that exploration. It begins with a look at the historical origins of the research paper in undergraduate education, and especially how the research paper genre began to make its appearance in composition textbooks. The second chapter examines student epistemologies, and how conventional research paper instruction sends students often conflicting messages about their role as knowers and their understanding of the nature of knowledge. In Chapter Three, I propose an alternative to the formal paper—the researched *essay*—which I argue is a far better introduction to research because it is more epistemologically sound, and more likely to encourage the habits of mind at the heart of academic inquiry. Finally, the last chapter examines the practical challenges of teaching a research essay in Freshman English.

A close examination of college writing texts—the focus of the next chapter—is revealing, not only because textbooks influenced how students represented the task of writing a term paper, but also, as Robert Connors has pointed out, because they "overwhelmingly shaped" our own theories and practices towards this assignment and others ("Textbooks" 178). How was the purpose of the research paper explained by these textbook authors? What was the relationship between this assignment and the other modes of student writing encouraged by college rhetorics?

If composition textbooks and the historical commitment to what Laurence Veysey calls the "research ideal" in American universities and colleges both contributed to conventional research paper instruction, then how have students and instructors internalized its aims? When my student Jayne, exasperated by my comments about her research paper in my office ten years ago, exclaimed, "This is a research paper, goddammit. It's supposed to be this way!", what she was really saying was that her paper was a performance that, in her mind, was already scripted. What is that script? What assumptions do students make about what it means to write a research paper, to read a source for it, to express an "opinion?" At the heart of these questions is one that seems central to much current debate in composition, and that I'll take up in Chapter Two: What does it mean to be a knower, and what is one's relationship to the known? Ever since Kenneth Burke gave us the conversation-filled parlor as the metaphor for participation in knowledge making, writing teachers have been debating the best ways to enable students to "put in their oar." That the freshman research paper has largely been ignored in this debate amazes me.[3] It is the one traditional assignment that most attempts to imitate academic discourse by exposing students to some other voices in the parlor. Most of us, when we assign the research paper, also expect students to speak up, to add their own voices to the hum of disciplinary conversation. One way of evaluating a particular pedagogy, then, is to ask whether it succeeds or fails in at least helping students *believe* that they can participate in the Burkean conversation.

Drawing on student papers, interviews, case studies, survey data, and my own experience as a writing teacher, I will argue that conventional research paper instruction has largely failed to move students towards the belief that they can be active knowers, or conscious participants in the making of knowledge, and that even when we encourage students to "think independently" or "express their own opinion" in less formal papers, they often do not understand what we mean. That we can "move" students at all towards more academic writing, particularly in a one- or even two-semester Freshman English course, is an assumption open to challenge. Almost fifteen years ago, Janet Emig (citing Howard Gruber) warned against "magical thinking," or the belief that teachers can take responsibility for their students' developments as writers. She wrote,

> Teachers of writing, for many reasons, have come to believe that children's learning to write is the direct outcome of their explicit teaching. Perhaps, because of massive public pressure, they have been forced to become the most magical thinkers of all. But what if, as evidence from many disciplines now suggests, writing is developmentally a *natural* process? What if "it is just as natural . . . to write books and to read them as it is natural to die or to be born?" (136)

For Emig, then, our challenge as writing teachers is to create the conditions that make this "natural" development of student writers possible, and to avoid the positivist belief that it is only through our instruction that we lead students to improvement. Though in later chapters I will offer some methods of instruction that I believe will help bring the freshman research paper back from the dead, much of this book focuses on the ways that the research paper has come to assume such an *unnatural* place in the composition course—that it has, in fact, disrupted the natural development of many student writers. Janet Emig argues that learning takes place in "an enabling environment," or one that is "safe, structured, unobtrusive, and literate," in which the teacher's role is as a "fellow practitioner" (139). Many contemporary composition courses, including my own, attempt to model these qualities—that is, until the last third of English 101 or in English 102 when students take up the research paper assignment. Suddenly, the course takes on a different tone, the instructor's role shifts, and much of what the students learned about writing in the first ten weeks of the class seems irrelevant.

Part of the problem, as Richard Larson points out in a much-cited essay, is that the freshman research paper is really a "non-form of writing." As Larson observes, it has evolved as a genre that is perceived to be separate from all the other writing that takes place in the composition course. In part, the freshman research paper's status as a separate genre is a result of its history. It is an assignment that has been dragged along into the modern writing process class as a vestige of now-discredited views of writing, and as a legacy of the service obligation to other departments with which freshman composition has long been burdened. But the research paper as an "unnatural" feature of Freshman

English also has to do with the tacit view that research is not a natural activity for any writer. I am often amazed, for example, at how rarely students view research as a revision strategy for a personal essay. Though my students often quickly see that writing is a means for exploring answers to meaningful questions, they have to be persuaded that reading or interviewing or field work is also a natural place to look for material. As Larson notes in his 1982 essay, "[r]esearch can inform virtually any writing or speaking if the author wishes it to do so."

> [T]here is nothing of substance or content that differentiates one paper that draws on data from outside the author's own self from another such paper—nothing that can enable one to say that this paper is a "research paper" and that paper is not. . . . If almost any paper is potentially a paper incorporating the fruits of research, the term "research paper" has virtually no value as an identification of a kind of substance in a paper. Conceptually, the generic term "research paper" is for practical purposes meaningless. (813)

What accounts for the widespread belief among our students that essays using "fact" as a source of information aren't essays? Why isn't research a natural source of information for all of the kinds of writing that go on in the composition course? Is it the fault of a dominant composition pedagogy that, as Robert Connors observed, has moved from the "outward-directed investigation" of classical rhetoric to the inward-looking personal writing assignment ("Personal Writing" 167)? Is Matthew Wilson right that "expressivist" pedagogies and the research paper are incompatible, making it difficult for students to "switch gears" from personal writing to more formal source-based writing (251)? Or have we been so careful to preserve the sanctity of The Research Paper, with our concerns about "objectivity," originality, and the meticulous following of conventions, that writing instructors have failed to see the assignment as a key bridge between the personal and the academic, and an opportunity for students to work out, in a meaningful way, their identities as knowers?

Ever since Jayne alerted me to my own failures with the research paper, I have revived it as the pivotal writing assignment in my Freshman English course. That has involved, among other things, demoting it as a separate genre and reintegrating it more naturally into the course. In later chapters I'll explore how this reconception of the so-called research paper genre demands that we confront a whole series of assumptions—many of them inherited uncritically—about what it means to be an academic researcher, including what Patricia Sullivan calls the "myth of the independent scholar," along with largely scientific notions of originality and objectivity.

But most important to my own rethinking of the research paper was the revelation that I had fenced off research in the academy from the research I had conducted as a professional writer for some years. I had failed to recognize what Huck knew instinctively: that while some of the conventions differ, all research is ultimately motivated by the same thing—curiosity.

It was an easy thing to forget. In *Common Ground*, Kurt Spellmeyer invokes the preindustrial commons as a metaphor for what was once the ideal of a "public language," and the university as a space where students and teachers might strive to speak it as a means of discovering differences—and commonalities—through open dialogue. It is this "public dimension" of academic life, one that is inclusive rather than exclusive, that invites a merging of the professional and the private, and encourages an "ethic of mutual understanding," that Spellmeyer argues has been lost by the fragmentation of the academy into separate disciplines with their own modes of thinking and talking. Freshman English is peculiarly positioned in all of this. As a required course that assembles a wide range of students with a variety of disciplinary interests (or none yet at all), first-year composition seems an ideal site to encourage the kind of dialogue Spellmeyer fears is lost. Instead, it is often a site of initiation in which the job of the writing teacher is to acquaint students with an academic landscape that is defined by differences rather than commonalities. "The history of writing instruction in America, or at least of writing instruction as we now practice it," writes Spellmeyer, "begins with an enclosure of our common linguistic ground—with the division of that ground into private parcels, each carefully fenced to exclude all trespassers" (7). Not only has the commons been fenced off, but in order to enter a private parcel, students are urged to shed their own ways of seeing and speaking so that they may see and speak like "us." Despite the promise that this will allow students to participate more fully in the Burkean conversation, Spellmeyer fears that it will have the opposite effect—that it will silence them:

> Through an encounter with the ways of seeing and acting that *our* language sustains, student-writers have the opportunity to enlarge their familiar worlds, and to appropriate our knowledge for their specific purposes. I believe, however, that conventional writing instruction more often produces the very opposite result: instead of opening the public dimension to our students, we set one language sharply at odds with the other—the correct against the incorrect, the high against the low. Obliged to choose, student-writers automatically lose both. Unable to be heard in the words they can claim as theirs, they learn to speak a language which remains the property of others. (6–7)

It is not too surprising, then, that along with my students I could so easily see the more public discourse of my own research writing as a creative writer separate from the discourse of academic research. Nor is it hard to see why I would dichotomize—along with my students—the work of an academic researcher and the research of a writer. One seems to be putting up fences, and the other is trying to tear them down.

I will argue in this book that the current move among some discourse theorists (or "New Formalists," as Spellmeyer describes them) to introduce students in the first-year composition course to the divided common by initiating them in the ways of disciplinary practices may have a result opposite from the one intended: It will undermine students' sense of agency rather than empower them, it will encourage submission rather than resistance, and it will promote a passive stance towards knowledge making rather than an active one. More specifically, I will make the case that Freshman English—and the research assignment in particular—are key sites where students *can* experience a more democratic relationship to what Bahktin calls "authoritative discourse," but only if they develop a faith in their own agency by seeing private experience and knowledge as a source of power and feel a sense of ownership over their own words.

While many students quickly see personal experience as a source of material for essays, and through personal writing many also experience as writers—often for the first time—a sense of authority over their subjects, when it comes to the research paper, students seem to disappear again. If subjectivity is celebrated in the personal essay, it is perceived as a fatal flaw in the research paper. Critics of expressivist pedagogy, like David Bartholomae, appear to argue that this is the way it should be. In "Inventing the University," he suggests that students earn the right to speak up in the parlor *after* they have practiced speaking and thinking like us. In essence, students must surrender their subjectivity, or at least the belief that they are in control of their own discourse, until they see how they are situated in the discourse of Others. He writes that "[i]t is difficult to imagine, however, how writers can have a purpose before they are located in a discourse, since it is the discourse with its projects and agendas that determines what writers can and will do" (139). In a more recent article, Bartholomae reiterates his contention that we must not conceal from our students "the power politics of discursive practice" ("Writing" 64) by creating the fiction that they are "free to express their own thoughts and ideas."

> Thinking of writing as academic writing makes us think of the page
> as crowded with others—or it says that this is what we learn in
> school, that our writing is not our own, nor are the stories we tell
> when we tell the stories of our lives—they belong to TV, to Books,
> to Culture and History. (63–4)

Though he never mentions the freshman research paper, Bartholomae seems to eloquently summarize *exactly* the lesson students have internalized through their experience with the assignment: that their writing is not their own. The result of this lesson is the stale, dishonest, lifeless writing that inspires writing teachers to pine for euthanasia and students to surf the Web to download someone else's paper. Mike Rose, Mina Shaugnessy, and others consider these failed experiments in trying out academic writing "a stage in linguistic growth." I see these failures reinforcing earlier experiences students have with research writing that undermines their belief in their ability to speak at all. I have tried to stake out two opposing positions that I think are important to this book. Both address this question: How do students learn more complex language and intellectual practices? One answer, provided by some discourse theorists, is that we encourage students, no matter how awkward it might seem, to imitate academic writing. The opposing answer, and the one I will attempt to develop at length here, is that students become academic writers by at first not yielding to authoritative discourse. And they do this by preserving a sense of self, a belief—even if it is a temporary fiction—that their writing *is* their own.

This is a debate that is being played out a great deal these days in composition journals and at conferences, but very few of the discussions take up the freshman research paper as a natural site for examining how students struggle with academic writing. After all, the term paper is the most common genre of student writing, and one that has historically purported to model academic discourse; it seems a likely place to look. Much of this work, then, focuses on the experience of student researchers. It will become apparent that even when students are encouraged to construct as sense of themselves as active knowers, as writers who own their words, they still often have difficulty with agency. In part, extended writing using sources imposes intellectual demands on inexperienced writers that makes it easy for them to lose themselves in another's discourse. We'll examine some of these demands. In addition, our own assumptions about the epistemelogical development of our students need to be reexamined: What do we assume about their sense of themselves as knowers, and what are our expectations about the ways the freshman research paper will change that sense? For example, when we ask students to "think independently" in their research papers, or to "express their own opinions," do they know what we mean? Do we?

More broadly speaking, what are reasonable aims for the freshman research paper? As Schwegler and Shamoon point out in their investigation of divergent views on the purpose of the assignment, many of these are directly contradictory. This book confirms some of their findings, including the observation that students by and large view the task as collecting and rearranging information, while instructors hope to encourage independent thought and interpretation. Is there a better way of articulating what we want students to do when they write a research paper? Can we redefine the aims of the assignment so that it's more meaningful to students, more likely to ultimately inspire more sophisticated intellectual practices? Is there some way to produce more Hucks and fewer Toms?

The most significant argument I'll make here concerning the aims of instruction is that we see the freshman research paper as less an introduction to the conventions and methods of academic writing and more as an opportunity to introduce students to the genuine spirit of inquiry, to certain habits of mind that often seem to inform investigations in many disciplines. The need to make "inquiry, investigation, and discovery . . . the heart of the enterprise" in the effort to revitalize American undergraduate education, particularly during the freshman year, was a central point of the Boyer Commission Report, a recent study by leading scholars and university officials ("Reinventing Undergraduate Education"). What better place to introduce this "shared mission" than in freshman composition—usually the one universally required course—and especially through the one assignment that is most common in that course: the research paper?

In the simplest terms, all inquiry is motivated by curiosity, a longing to know that will sustain the researcher through the inevitable conflicts, contradictions, and frustrations that are part of the search. It is the ability, in John Dewey's terms, "to protract that state of doubt which is the stimulus to thorough inquiry" (16) that marks the thoughtful researcher, and it is exactly that ability which students have been denied through traditional research instruction. Though even the earliest composition texts encourage students to choose a topic for research that interests them, the traditional emphasis on "objectivity," originality, formal conventions, argument, and the need to write a thesis-driven text mitigates against Dewey's protracted state of doubt. Students rightly infer that "getting it right" is far more important than getting confused.

Ultimately, what drives the conventional freshman research paper is not the writer's curiosity, but the compulsion to imitate (or parody?) a conception of formal academic writing, and a key part of that conception is surrendering a sense of themselves as authors of their own work. "I feel as though when I'm writing a research paper and I'm researching it and writing, and it's three o'clock in the morning and it's due in five hours . . . you're really not thinking of yourself as a writer," Kate Carter, a college senior told me as she reflected on her experience writing term papers. "You think of yourself more as a researcher." Though she didn't elaborate on it, Kate's distinction between being a "writer" and being a "researcher" implies two different ways of being in the world—a writer creates, while a researcher collects?—each occupying separate domains. This separation of the act of writing and researching, and the role of the writer and researcher, is the result of a failed term paper pedagogy that extends beyond the Freshman English course. But I will argue that the first-year writing course ought to be the place where students get practice being writers who ask questions that research can help answer. I propose that we expose the artificial distinctions between writer and researcher, writing and researching that conventional pedagogy reinforces. The researched *essay*, not the research paper, is much more likely to erase these distinctions.

In addition, we must teach an approach to research writing that places it in the domain most important to the writer and her general reader—it must have, as the pragmatist William James put it, "some positive connexion with this actual world of finite human lives" (17). When a sense of authorship is effaced, it is easy for students to conclude that the research paper has nothing to do with their lives. Worse, they may come to believe that research writing has nothing to do with life; instead, students view it as a form of writing incubated in the insular and sterile region of school concerned with "fact," having little to do with their hopes, fears, longings, sorrows, and joys. In the pedagogy proposed in the third and fourth chapters, I will contend that the best way to introduce students to the spirit of inquiry and the genuine nature of research is to encourage them to explore questions that arise from their lived experience and to test whatever ideas they discover against the pragmatist's central question, as posed by James:

> Grant an idea or belief to be true . . . what concrete difference will
> its being true make in anyone's actual life? How will the truth be
> realized? What experiences will be different from those which
> would obtain if the belief were false? What, in short, is the truth's
> cash-value in experiential terms? (97)

Though James gives these questions a philosophical spin, they are really the questions any good writer might ask himself when considering material: How does this subject matter to me, and how can I help my readers see that it matters to them?

More than ten years ago I began work on a nonfiction book on the American lobster. *The Lobster Almanac* was an exploration of the animal's natural history, cultural and economic status in New England, and culinary qualities. The book was published in 1988, several years after I had Jayne in my summer section of Freshman English. It was that project that finally convinced me that I had failed Jayne and the many students who came before her in my writing classes. I had failed to teach them that research is not the soul-killing exercise many of them imagined it to be, and that "fact" need not deaden prose. I had failed to help them to see that research and research-based writing can be a *pleasure*; it is work, too, of course, but frequently filled with moments when, through the reading, the writing, and the talking, an unexpected door opens on the subject and the light suddenly pours in. Though it may make me, in Tom Sawyer's words, a "perfect saphead," I believe that this promise of pleasure is what we must teach most of all in a renewed research paper pedagogy.

Beyond Note Cards: Rethinking the Freshman Research Paper does not offer the published scholarship of the academic as the most instructive models of research writing for the first-year student. Too often the pleasures and passions of the academic for her subject are masked by the carefully choreographed dance of discourse. Instead, I propose that the works of essayists and journalists such as John McPhee, Diane Ackerman, Richard Conniff, Ann Hodgman, and Barry Lopez are the best introductions to the spirit of inquiry that drives all research, and that facts, in the hands of a good writer, can also inspire the pleasures of personal discovery.

Some years before Mark Twain wrote *Huckleberry Finn*, he learned the Mississippi River as a river boat captain. It was, he wrote in *Life on the Mississippi*, a mixed blessing to come to know the river this way. While he had "mastered the language of the water" (quoted in Sanders, "Speaking" 218), recognizing the distinctive swirls of a snag and the subtle color of the shallows, he admitted that he also "lost something which could never be restored to me while I lived": the river's beauty, its grace, and its poetry. As Scott Sanders observes, Twain was not quite right about that. Several years later, the author finds in Huck a way to "fuse an adult's rational knowledge and a child's fresh emotion in his vision of the river" ("Speaking" 218).

In our rush to initiate students in "our" discourses through the formal research paper, it may seem that they have much to gain: They will acquire more complex language, and more sophisticated critical skills that will help them succeed in school. I believe, however, that they have much more to lose. In our rush to make them river boat captains, they will learn to disengage themselves from knowledge and the act of inquiry, from the ways of knowing that we want to encourage. They *can* learn what Twain demonstrates in *Huckleberry Finn*: Learning the language of the river need not mean sacrificing a fresh, and personal, vision of it. In short, we can teach our students to be *both* Hucks and riverboat captains. But only if we don't make an immediate ascent to the pilot house a condition of the journey.

Notes

1. A number of states, including Massachusetts and Texas, have made term paper sales over the Internet illegal if the vendor knowingly facilitates student plagiarism, something that is no doubt difficult to prove. In the fall of 1997, Boston University also filed a federal lawsuit against a number of the online companies, charging them with wire fraud, mail fraud, and racketeering. BU invited other schools to join the suit.

2. In her 1958 study, Ambrose Manning broke down her results by region as well. She found that the required research paper was a particular popular assignment in the West (90.9 percent require it) and the Southeast (90 percent), and least popular in the Northeast (55 percent), a region she speculated was "leading the way in eliminating the research project in Freshman English." It was not a prophetic comment, obviously.

3. One notable exception to this is Douglas Brent's recent book, *Reading as Rhetorical Invention*. Though it is an important and thoughtful work, Brent's text focuses largely on a rhetoric of reading and its implications for research paper pedagogy. *Beyond Note Cards* looks more closely at the difficulties student writers have as knowers, and the ways that conventional research paper instruction often compound their difficulties.

One

A Captive Genre
The Rise and Fall of the "Source Theme"

Two things occurred in the past few years that I later realized were telling commentaries on the current state of academic research and how it is perceived by non-academics. While I was attending a panel at the Modern Language Association convention, a member of the audience rose during a question-and-answer session, clutching a sheaf of papers, photocopies of a *Los Angeles Times* article that appeared the day before. The article condemned the obtuse language and imponderable paper topics that dominated a convention of professional English teachers. The MLA member in the audience that day was indignant at the anti-intellectual slant of the piece, but also worried that the profession seems so misunderstood. Kurt Spellmeyer, a panel member and a composition theorist, pointed out that perhaps we are misunderstood because we have become unwilling to make ourselves understood. Perhaps, he said, what we do seems to have no visible relation to people's lives.

The following month I had a phone conversation with my mother. "Did you see the 'Sixty Minutes' piece last night on academia?" she said. I hadn't. But, in the ensuing weeks, I heard about it from several students, a real estate agent, a dental hygienist, and several colleagues, one of whom was an adjunct faculty member with six years in my department. I bumped into her at a bookstore, and, taking her cue from the "Sixty Minutes" piece, she said, "Can you believe that the library spends millions of dollars buying academic journals that nobody reads just so professors can publish their indecipherable articles in them so they can get tenure?" The implication was, among other things, that the money might be better spent paying adjunct faculty more to teach composition. I nodded sympathetically but walked away feeling ambivalent. *I read many of those journals, I thought, and not all of them are indecipherable, and what does Leslie Stahl really know about academic life anyway?* But the two incidents—my experience at the MLA a few years ago and my colleague's comments—also reinforced a sense that something is profoundly amiss with academic scholarship and its relevance to nonspecialists, even to those who exist within the academy and teach academic writers.

The problem, argues history professor Patricia Nelson Limerick, is a system of graduate education that "enforce(s) a standard of dull writing." She writes that professors "demand dreariness because they think dreariness is in the students' best interests" (23). To illustrate her point, Limerick invokes an amusing anecdote about trying to get buzzards to fly on cue during the production of *Hud*, a film starring Paul Newman. During the buzzard scene, the script called for the birds to all roost ominously in a tree until Newman fired a shot, and then take flight simultaneously. Buzzards being buzzards, not actors, they wouldn't stay in the tree, so the technicians concluded that they could wire the birds' feet to the branches and release them all at once when the gun was fired. Unfortunately, the buzzards, denied flight, all decided that the only alternative was not to sit quietly waiting for their cue, but to fall forward and hang upside down, flapping in frustration. Upside-down buzzards apparently present physiological problems. They all passed out after a few moments of frantic wing beats.

This was obviously not what the movie makers had in mind. Nor were the birds too keen on it. After being repeatedly revived and set back on their branches, the birds stopped falling forward, but when their wires were released, they wouldn't budge. As Limerick puts it on behalf of the buzzards, "We *tried* that before. It did not work. We are not going to try it again" (23). She writes,

> How does this parable apply? In any and all disciplines, you go to graduate school to have your feet wired to the branch. There is nothing inherently wrong with that: scholars should have some common ground, share some background assumptions, hold some similar habits of mind. This gives you, quite literally, your footing. And yet, in the process of getting your feet wired, you have some awkward moments, and the intellectual equivalent of pitching forward and hanging upside down. . . . One or two rounds of that humiliation, and the world begins to seem like a very treacherous place. Under those circumstances, it does indeed seem to be the choice of wisdom *to sit quietly on the branch*, to sit without even the *thought* of flying, since even the thought might be enough to tilt the

balance and set off another round of flapping, fainting, and embarrassment. (23)

Even when scholars emerge from graduate school and are free to fly, Limerick argues, they never leave the branch, and in turn when they teach *their* graduate students academic conventions, what these new professors instill is a fear of flying, a reluctance to depart from the "dreary" writing that they have come to believe is "an academic survival skill." What she indicts is not simply the "awful writing style" (24) of the academic writer, but the ways in which those linguistic conventions, invoked as a means of protecting the writer from criticism, shut out a more general readership from the work of the academy.

Limerick's essay itself may be a demonstration of some of the pitfalls of an academic writer going public, particularly on the subject of scholarly research. Her sweeping characterization of academic discourse as "dreary" and wholly inaccessible is an appealing condemnation to those inclined to agree, but as David Bartholomae has pointed out, "academic writing is a single thing only in convenient arguments" ("Writing" 62). But there is evidence, including the growing resistance of state legislatures to adequately fund public universities, that scholarship is increasingly perceived by the public as remote, irrelevant, and even frivolous. It now falls to the university public relations department to somehow translate the specialized scholarship of the modern university into terms that nonspecialists can understand. Limerick and composition theorists, such as Spellmeyer, contend that we shouldn't leave it entirely to the public relations office to articulate the significance of academic research. It is not only possible, but also desirable that academic writers embrace a more public dimension in their work. Limerick argues that

> [t]he redemption of the university, especially in terms of the public's appraisal of the value of research and publication, requires all writers who have something they want to publish to ask themselves the question: Does this have to be a closed communication, shutting out all but specialists willing to fight their way through the thickets of jargon? Or can this be an open communication, engaging specialists with new information and new thinking, but also offering an invitation to nonspecialists to learn from this study, to grasp its importance and, by extension, to find concrete reasons to see value in the work of the university? (23–4)

The great difficulty academic researchers have taking Limerick's advice, negotiating successfully between two seemingly different languages—the public and the specialized—is exactly the difficulty student writers face in Freshman English when they tackle the research paper. Who am I writing for, they wonder? How much should I assume my readers know? How formal should the paper be, and how technical should I get? To what extent must I follow academic rules to demonstrate I'm entitled to membership even at the risk of losing my sense of self? Should I sit quietly on the branch, or should I fly?

What I want to suggest in this chapter is that the struggles of academic writers—both experienced and inexperienced—with negotiating the specialized discourses of disciplines and the public discourses of a democratic culture have their origins in the transformation of the American university in the last century. In particular, the "ideal of research," inspired largely by the example of German scholarship in the late nineteenth century and later embraced by academics in the United States, has been largely responsible for turning students into buzzards and the freshman research paper into the carrion upon which they first feed. As Kurt Spellmeyer points out, Freshman English occupied a unique position as the American academy became increasingly fragmented into separate disciplines and departments.

> Freshman English . . . owed its very existence to the growth of specialization—to the assumption that "writing" occupied a specific place along the modern disciplinary spectrum, comfortably positioned, one might suppose, somewhere between business administration and psychology. But while teachers of writing continued to believe that their "art" was indeed universal, the pace of change made it harder and harder for them to deny what everyone else saw clearly: just as each discipline had its own mode of practice, each had its own mode of discourse as well. In this lay their professional dilemma, for once language no longer reaffirmed the existence of a "world" greater than the differences named— once language seemed only to offer further evidence of a total fragmentation—freshman English abruptly became a discipline devoted to nothing in particular, a field without a subject, a methodology without a method. (*Common Ground* 17)

If Spellmeyer is right when he contends that many of the competing composition pedagogies that have emerged in the last thirty years all attempt to address this loss of belief in the universality of language to unite knowledge rather than divide it, then the research paper— perhaps more than any form of writing in the first-year course—becomes a site of conflict. It is, after all, the form that is most associated with specialized writing and knowledge. It is also the genre that emerged as an explicit model of academic writing that students are urged to imitate. Finally, if writing teachers came to suspect that they occupy a "field without a subject"—that, somehow, when the commons got divided up among the disciplines, they didn't get any turf— then one solution is to devote oneself to serving those who do. The obligation Freshman English instructors feel to provide a service to other disciplines is one important factor that explains the persistence of the freshman research paper, despite the dread it inspires.

To understand the often conflicting (and often unstated) aims of the research paper, and the ways in which it has been isolated as a separate form of writing, one must see it as an historical relic. It has been shaped by several forces: the emergence of the research ideal in American universities, the shifting relationship of the first-year writing course to the increasingly specialized academic community that surrounds it, and the discrediting of a rhetoric of public discourse for an essentially arhetorical view of writing in which the language that serves fact is viewed as transparent and objective.

Because of its history, the freshman research paper has always had an uneasy relationship with those charged to teach it. English teachers are torn between their obligation to school students in research practices for other departments and their own commitments to writing as an aesthetic or expressive act. They often do not sense, given their implicit understanding of the genre, that there isn't necessarily a conflict between the research paper and the personal essay. The inherited legacy of the research ideal does not prepare them to see that there can be a "literature of fact,"[1] research writing that is both, in James Britton's terms, "expressive" *and* "transactional." Finally, both the epistemological assumptions of the research ideal, and the research paper pedagogies that have grown from them, have made it difficult for English teachers to fit the assignment into the writing process class. As a result, the research paper in both Freshman English and high school writing classes often seems like a lingering dinosaur that somehow survived the near extinction of current–traditional rhetoric.

This chapter offers some historical reasons why, in Richard Larson's words, the "so-called 'research paper' has no conceptual or substantive identity" (813) and why our traditional approaches to teaching it in the English department are "not defensible" (812). I first examine a cluster of beliefs and assumptions about the assignment shared by students in a freshman writing program, and then trace the origins of those beliefs to textbook treatments of the freshman research paper and to the changes in the American university beginning in the late nineteenth century and into the twentieth. I end this chapter with a call for reconceiving the assignment based in part on a rejection of some of our inherited notions of the research ideal. But I also argue that history offers us a way to see a reconceived freshman research paper as part of a rhetorical tradition that S. Micheal Halloran argues should be revived: a rhetoric that contributes to a public discourse, not a specialized one. The research paper can be an assignment that actively encourages students to consider the public dimension of their investigations, one that is "in essence a rhetoric of citizenship" (Halloran 108). If the history of research paper instruction tells the story of how to wire the buzzard's feet, the rhetorical tradition may also remind us of a way to set them free.

Reading the Script

What *do* our students believe they are being asked to do when given a research paper assignment? What assumptions do they make about how they should approach it, and how do they represent the teacher's expectations of the task? Are these student assumptions at odds with our own sense of why we teach the research paper? I have long sensed that at the heart of the widespread complaints about the freshman research paper among instructors is a feeling of disappointment—the belief that students somehow failed to meet instructors' expectations of a meaningful inquiry and the compelling paper that arises from it. Students often recognize this disappointment and, like my own former student Jayne, respond to it with frustration. What seems obvious in this cycle of disappointment and frustration is a disparity between student assumptions about the assignment—its aims and its methods—and our own. When we assign a research paper, do students understand its purpose in the same way we do?

I don't think so. While an exploration of the purposes and methods of the freshman research paper have consumed remarkably little ink in composition journals, one 1982 article by Robert Schwegler and Linda Shamoon addresses the subject directly. Based on interviews with instructors and students, the authors conclude that the two groups have "substantially different attitudes toward the research process and the aim, forms, and audience of the research paper" (818). Schwegler and Shamoon conclude that

> Students view the research paper as a close-ended, informative, skills-oriented exercise written for an expert audience by novices pretending to be experts. . . . Academics, on the other hand, view the research paper as open-ended and interpretive, written for an audience of fellow inquirers who have specific expectations of logic, structure and style. Academic research papers reflect this view by being narrowly focused, aware of the scholarly audience, and frequently tentative in advancing a conclusion. (820)

In an effort to update and expand the Shamoon and Schwegler study, I surveyed students in the University of New Hampshire composition program to examine the cluster of beliefs and assumptions that guide students when they are assigned a research paper. I gave a similar survey to a small group of their instructors.[2] The results of the survey will also be explored in Chapter Two, but the first two sections—how students represent themselves as writers of research papers and how they represent the assignment—shed light on some of the sources of teacher disappointment and student frustration with research writing. The results suggest that students and their instructors do not share much common ground.

What struck me first about the instructors' responses to questions about the assignment's purpose and their expectations was the positive language most used. When the teachers were asked to "list briefly your three most important aims in assigning" a freshman research paper, two respondents expressed their hope that students would find research "*fun* or *exciting*," or that they would learn "the *joy* of investigating topic of interest." Another hoped the assignment would "help students to wonder—remind them that wanting to know why is *good*, *noble*, important." A fourth hoped students would see that "the knowledge we gain from research can be used as a *creative* tool," and that the resulting paper would be "thoughtful, engaging, and if possible, *fun*." And a fifth respondent emphasized "the *satisfaction* of finding out they knew more than they thought they knew." Only one instructor—the teacher who ranked the assignment the lowest of the nine respondents in terms of its importance in his course—described the research paper in negative terms, and even that was somewhat mixed. When asked what he expects students to do when assigned a research paper, the instructor wrote that they will be "either pissed or elated; they either hate to do the work or love RP's because they can 'crank them out without a problem.'"

What accounts for the positive cast these instructors placed on the freshman research paper? In part it reflects the somewhat unique nature of the UNH freshman writing program, with its "expressivist" orientation and the tendency among its practitioners to share the belief that writing is an act of self-discovery. The instructors' hopeful attitude about the research paper might also represent a belief, widely shared among those within the academy, that inquiry and research is a valued and valuable activity, not only an essential part of academic life, but also one that provides personal gratification. Whatever the reason for the attitude among these instructors, it stands in contrast to the views of many students towards the assignment. Of the 196 students responding to the open-ended question, "When you're given an assignment to write a research paper, what do you assume you're being asked to do?", very few used the positive language expressed by their instructors. Most students simply described the task. (For example, the most common description was that the assignment involves exclusively library work, an assumption I think we need to challenge.) But when another survey question prompted students to characterize the research paper by using an analogy, it was often negative:

- "Kinda like being a vacuum"
- "Like an encyclopedia that keeps going on and on"
- "A blind man walking down the street without his cane—he'll stumble along and maybe he'll find something"
- "An entertainer on stage, a comic trying to get through my routine on paper"
- "An atheist going to church on Sunday"

Even more revealing is the disparity between instructor and student assumptions about the nature of the assignment. In the survey, I listed sixteen statements about the research paper assignment or the act of researching and asked respondents to check those that were consistent with their own assumptions about both. These statements ranged from those that reflected assumptions about how papers should be written—"Can't use 'I'" or "Form matters more than content"—to statements about the research process and the rhetorical situation—"Information should come mostly from books" or "It's okay to say things the instructor might disagree with." (See Table 1–1 for the complete list.)

Though the small sample size of teachers who participated in the survey exaggerates the results somewhat, I was struck by the number of assumptions about the assignment that teachers and students don't share at all. For example, half of the items that were checked by 20 percent or more of the students in the study were ignored completely by their instructors. Of these, several assumptions were shared by 50 percent or more of the students surveyed, including the belief that use of the first person isn't allowed in the research paper (57 percent), that it must "follow a formal structure" (69 percent), that books are the primary source of information (52 percent), and that research papers "have to be objective" (60 percent). In fact, the only area of substantial agreement between students and instructors is the view that "it's okay to say things the instructor might not agree with." Another striking disparity between the two groups centers on whether students are "supposed to use their own opinions" in a research paper. While all nine instructors surveyed indicated that students should use their opinions, just over 20 percent, or only one-fifth of the students surveyed, shared that view.

The survey, which was conducted before the instructors had done much, if any, research paper instruction, largely reflects the attitudes that many students bring with them to college. Presumably all of the instructors surveyed would expect that at least some of these views would change by the end of the semester. But based on the results of this survey, these attitudes often appear to persist among students

Table 1–1.   Results of Part II of Survey
"When you're given an assignment to write a research paper, which of
the following do you generally assume about it?"

Item	% Checked
A. I can't use "I."	57
B. My information should come mostly from books.	52
C. I can use my own experiences and observations as evidence.	55
D. I have to know my thesis before I start.	60
E. I'm supposed to use my own opinions.	22
F. Summarizing what's known about the topic is most important.	36
G. I have to try to say something original.	43
H. I need to follow a formal structure.	69
I. The instructor probably knows more than I do about the topic.	22
J. I can write in my own writing voice.	37
K. I'm writing exclusively for the instructor.	23
L. I'm supposed to make an argument.	42
M. The paper won't be revised substantially.	15
N. Form matters more than content.	10
O. It's okay to say things the instructor might disagree with.	85
P. I have to be objective.	60

who have written two or more term papers in other college classes
during their freshman year. While composition instructors may be
committed to challenging the beliefs their students hold about the research paper, teachers in other disciplines don't seem to influence
those beliefs much at all, at least during the freshman year.

To get a broad picture of student assumptions about the research
assignment, Table 1–1 reports the percentage of students checking
each of the sixteen statements in Part II of the survey. The results will
be mostly unsurprising to composition instructors. Aside from the beliefs that researchers must be "objective," write papers that follow a
formal structure, avoid use of the first person, and use mostly books
as sources, 60 percent of the respondents believe that they must *begin*
the research process with a thesis, confirming Schwegler and
Shamoon's earlier finding that students view research as a "closed end
process." Just over 40 percent agreed that they have to "say some-

thing original" in their papers and construct an argument. All of these are assumptions that might naturally grow from conventional research paper instruction.[3] Some are beliefs that many instructors might endorse, even if those in this survey do not.

In later chapters I argue that many of these attitudes undermine students' understanding of the genuine nature of inquiry, alienate them from the process, and often frustrate our aim of encouraging students to become active knowers. But first, what *is* conventional research paper instruction, and where might these persistent assumptions about the research paper genre originate?

No More Than Paste-pot and Shears

"During the eighteenth, nineteenth, and early twentieth centuries," writes Robert Connors, "composition theory and pedagogy were overwhelmingly shaped by one great force: textbooks" ("Textbooks" 178). Though its historical roots may be in rhetoric, composition's "practical pedagogy" owes its greatest debt, says Connors, to the proliferation of textbooks, particularly in the latter part of the nineteenth century and the first thirty or forty years of the twentieth. As a young field (many date its genuine beginning to the early 1960s), composition for many years lacked "the usual disciplinary balance between journals and textbooks" (190), and the result is that the textbook, particularly in the hands of the inexperienced or disinterested writing teacher, became both a source of knowledge and a means of knowledge making. That this was especially the case during the period that the freshman research paper first made its appearance (often in the guise of another name) highlights the crucial significance of the composition text as a parent of the assignment. How the genre is now conceived by students and teachers alike cannot be divorced from its evolution on the pages of books such as Slater's 1922 edition of *Freshman Rhetoric* or Baker and Haller's 1929 edition of *Writing: A First Book for College Students* or the influential 1941 edition of the *Harbrace College Handbook* (Hodges).

In *Writing in the Academic Disciplines: 1870–1990*, David Russell observes that the "[t]erm paper has rarely been studied and even more rarely studied as a genre worthy of historical analysis" (78). Though his text offers the most extended analysis of the origins of the research paper, Russell devotes only several paragraphs to its treatment in composition textbooks. As part of this study, I examined roughly fifty composition textbooks, most published since 1900. Earlier texts, including the three that dominated the market in the latter part of the nineteenth century—A.S. Hill's *Principles of Rhetoric* (1878), John Genung's *Practical Elements of*

Rhetoric (1886), and Barrett Wendell's *English Composition* (1891)—all lack any references to writing with sources, much less mention the "source theme" or "term paper" as a genre of student writing.[4]

One reason for the absence of source-based writing instruction in texts before 1900 may be the still-limited nature of university library collections at the end of the nineteenth century and well into the twentieth. By 1875 no American colleges, except Harvard, had anything approaching a "university library," and annual acquisitions at most schools numbered only in the hundreds (Danton 31). What books could be found in these libraries were considered too valuable to lend out, and they were guarded zealously, often locked in cabinets, by college librarians. This lock-and-leave approach to books in academic libraries remained largely unchallenged until 1876, when the U.S. Department of Education published a study of the country's public libraries, advocating freer use of books by students despite the risks, a move library historian Arthur Hamlin called "the single most important event in the history of the American academic library" (23).

Growth of academic libraries, however, was slow. Harvard's collection, the nation's first and largest major college library, numbered only 84,200 volumes in 1850. Fifty years later, the collection was over a half million, but by 1920—the period when methods of library research began to appear in composition textbooks—the Harvard library had four times that number of books in its collection (Danton 20, 87, 91). In 1930–1931 alone, Harvard's Widener Library acquired more than 193,000 volumes (Wilson, "Service of Libraries" 130). No other state or private university, with the exception of Yale, even approached half the number of books in Harvard's collection until 1940. Not coincidentally, the forties was the decade when the freshman research paper increasingly received its own chapter in a growing number of writing texts.

Despite the inadequacy of university libraries, early composition teachers and rhetoricians often promoted wide reading of ancient and contemporary classics as a source of information for freshman themes, and familiarity with methods of library research as a fundamental skill. According to Robert Connors, even late nineteenth century composition instructors recognized that their students could "easily . . . come up with an essay essentially cribbed from secondary sources" (*Composition-Rhetoric* 321), a concern that also led to the rise of the research paper as a genre. He cites two other reasons for the genre's emergence: increased concern by the beginning of the twentieth century with protecting intellectual property—avoiding plagiarism—and a reaction among some composition instructors to the growing popularity of personal writing in the course. Nothing was viewed as more impersonal than the research paper (323).

But the first and most influential public voice for the freshman research paper was not in the nineteenth century but in the twentieth. Charles Sears Baldwin wrote in 1906 that "from the beginning a student should learn that his use of the library will be a very practical measure of his culture" ("Freshman English" 486). For Baldwin, an authority on classical rhetoric, Freshman English should train the student not only in rhetorical methods of presentation, but also in the means of investigation, so that "he brings his studies in closer relation to himself."

> This idea naturally leads to the library. For freshman composition may involve reading, not only in study of models, but also practice in compilation. Minds accustomed to accept and repeat generalizations at second hand may be taught, not only to reflect, but also, within feasible limits, to investigate. How to find facts, how to compare inferences, and finally how to bring reading to bear,—in all this, freshman composition may be of *practical service* to any other course, and of liberal service to the student himself. That compilation is commonly regarded as a mechanical process of paste-pot and shears, when experience proves it to be, *not only open to originality, but in many cases positively conducive to originality*, is a reminder to freshman English. (*A College Manual* 489; emphasis is mine)

Several notions that will later have profound implications for research paper instruction surface here: that library skills are a "practical service" freshman composition can provide the rest of the university, and that students can conduct *original* investigations using library sources. Baldwin later expands these in his popular 1906 textbook, *A College Manual of Rhetoric,* the earliest textbook I've found that deals at length with writing essays based on research.

Baldwin's text, typical of the many freshman writing texts that followed in the next twenty years, describes the researched essay not as a separate genre but as a form of exposition. *A College Manual* divides rhetoric into "logical composition," which includes persuasion and exposition and has its theory in ancient rhetoric, and "literary composition," which includes narration and description and has its foundation in ancient poetics. (This division may later influence the inability of writing teachers to see anything aesthetic about fact-based writing.) Under exposition, Baldwin identifies two types: essays based on personal experience and those based on reading. Here again he emphasizes the ideal of "originality of compilation" in researched expository essays, noting that while it "deals commonly with material already known" the "result may be original . . . whenever a writer gives to facts, however often they may have been presented, his own grouping and interpretation" (39).

> This kind of writing of writing is at once directly educative in
> college and directly useful outside. Originality of discovery, as in
> science, originality of creation, as in art, are for most men equally
> impossible; but originality of compilation, the power to read facts,
> to analyze, to collate, combine them, to give them promptly such
> direction as shall unfold their significance, is a mastery hardly to
> be shirked by any educated man. To energize knowledge is the
> office of persuasion; but to realize knowledge comes first, and this
> is the office of exposition. (39–40)

Later in this chapter I explore how the research ideal in the modern American university gave the notion of originality a particular weight and cast, but notice how Baldwin struggles with his own conception of how it applies to the student research essay. While denying "most men" the "originality of discovery" or the "originality of creation," he celebrates the more available talent of "originality of compilation." But what does this mean? Assembling, analyzing, and arranging others' facts to "unfold their significance" does not sound too different from what Baldwin described as the "paste-pot and shears" method he condemns elsewhere. It is possible, of course, that it is not only the "grouping," but also the writer's own "interpretation" of the facts that is original, but as with so many of the texts I examined, the sample research essay Baldwin includes in his book seems to subvert many of his claims about originality. The Appendix of *A College Manual of Rhetoric* includes "an example of simple research" (264)—a student's notes and his or her resulting essay on the Roman infantry. The essay is the familiar encyclopedic summary of facts with no explicit evidence of the writer's interpretation save the very last line of the essay: "No wonder the Roman legion was an effective fighting machine" (269).

Baldwin's struggle to establish a principle of originality that would apply to the research essay is one that we will see repeated again and again in later texts; it remains a vexing problem for contemporary writing teachers and students.[5] In many other ways *A College Manual of Rhetoric* establishes a precedent for textbook treatment of research-based writing. Baldwin's text appears to be the first to feature extended discussion of note-taking methods—including the earliest reference to the ubiquitous note cards ("small slips or cards")—and the first to offer an extensive list of topics for research (49). For example, the appendix includes ten pages of suggested topics, in categories ranging from "reports and other essays based on personal observation and current reading, especially of newspapers" to suggested topics for "essays supported by elementary research" to appropriate topics for "longer essays for advanced students" (253–63). Among the topics for long investigative essays were these: the Holy Grail, "some American literary traditions," Oxford, romantic music, and the American whaleman.

For the next fifteen years, Baldwin's *College Manual* was the only major freshman writing text to provide such a full treatment of bibliographic methods and the researched essay. By the 1920s, however, textbook treatments of library research began to proliferate. A typical example is Carson's 1920 *Handbook of English Composition*, which features a detailed description of how to prepare bibliographic material and use note cards, as well as a list of key references students should consult. Greenough and Hersey's *English Composition* (1924) opens with a chapter titled, "Gathering and Weighing Material." It includes sections on use of the library and suggestions for reading, "weighing authorities," note taking, "being original," and "why you must not copy without acknowledgment." The dangers of plagiarism are mentioned in virtually all of the early textbook discussions of the research essay, though a detailed description of methods of citation—footnotes and the like—did not appear in the books I examined until the 1930s. The note card became a permanent resident of the library research chapters in 1920 textbooks, and perhaps the earliest specialized text on research skills, Leonard and Fuess' *Practical Precis Writing*, appeared in 1929. Using mostly passages of verse ranging from easy to difficult, this text elevated summarizing to a new status. "The mere practice of precis writing," the authors proclaim, "trains the mind to seize on what is essential and to disregard what is subordinate or merely decorative in writing. A month's course in the writing of summaries in the classroom will seldom fail to develop a proficiency which will be of immense value" (14).

Though virtually all of the composition texts published in the 1920s feature very similar treatments of research writing—describing it as a form of exposition, detailing library research methods, discussing the need for originality, and emphasizing the practical value of research skills—I did discover one text that was a notable exception. Baker and Haller's *Writing: A First Book for College Students* (1929) is a text that guides students through a semester-long research project on a topic of their choice, culminating in a long investigative theme. Rather than writing a number of shorter essays on "unrelated topics," Baker and Haller suggest that the student read "widely and thoroughly on a topic about which he is curious, and which he has chosen independently for its own sake" (iv). While almost every textbook I examined urged students to choose topics that they find interesting, Baker and Haller return to the theme again and again: "With almost any bit of writing that is really worthwhile, what starts the writer is curiosity. . . . Curiosity is probably one of the chief reasons why you have come to college. . . . College is, therefore, a kind of curiosity disposal plant. It matters little what you are curious about so long as you are curious" (4–5, 7). While the need to conduct "original" investigations also surfaces in Baker and Haller's textbook, in a significant break with books that preceded and followed them, the authors suggest that it is experience—not merely a fresh arrangement of material culled from library sources—that will give student research papers originality: "Put your present knowledge to work. Think up some way which you can do some original investigation, make some first-hand observation of the facts of your subject. In other words, *go and see for yourself*" (93; emphasis is mine).

Though *Writing: A First Book for College Students* could be considered simply an anomaly, I think its treatment of the investigative theme is significant for several reasons. First, though its authors briefly mention that its method was "inaugurated in principle" (v) by Charles Sears Baldwin in his work at Barnard years before (something my investigation of Baldwin's work does not suggest), the text seems to be the only one I examined that was influenced by the progressive education movement that was transforming American schools at the time. In particular, Baker and Haller's emphasis on research projects that are student initiated, grounded in experience, and shift the teacher's role from taskmaster to guide are some of the key elements of Dewey-inspired educational theory, which coalesced in the creation of the Progressive Education Association in 1919. The organization reached the peak of its influence in the late 1920s (Cremin). *Writing: A First Book for College Students* is also worthy of note because it is ancestor to a research paper pedagogy that finds later expression in Kenneth Macrorie's *The I-Search Paper* and my own text, *The Curious Researcher*. Baker and Haller's book represents an alternative tradition to conventional research paper instruction, which I attempt to theorize and extend in this book.

One way in which Baker and Haller's text echoes all of the others I examined that were published during the twenties is the emphasis on a research essay intended for a general reader, an obvious implication of making it a category of exposition, rather than a specialized genre. The rhetorical structure of the assignment begins to change, however, in 1930s' composition texts. Textbook authors increasingly described the research paper as the product of serious scholarship, a distinct genre with a specialized audience whose purpose is to extend and build knowledge. Howard Baldwin's *Handbook of Modern Writing* (1930), for example, is careful to distinguish between writing "only a few centuries ago" when the task was to collect and arrange quotations from "ancient authors"—a method "comparable to assembling an automobile from parts manufactured by various companies"—and the "radically changed" approach to writing in which the writer "should if possible discover some neglected phase of the subject, some new meaning in the facts, or some novel manner of presentation" (5). Bryan, Nethercot, and De Voto's *Writer's Handbook* (1931), in a separate chapter "Preparation of Papers," mentions the research paper as a "serious, informative article" that should carefully follow "the methods of serious scholars" (216). Increasingly, *term paper* is used in these texts to describe the genre, perhaps reflecting its increasing use in all disciplines. The term paper's chief aim, according to one 1930 survey of faculty, was "to increase the student's knowledge of a *special* field" (Brown and Baldwin 307; emphasis is mine). As always, the emphasis on originality or independent thought remains, but now it is more couched in the language of the "research ideal"—the responsibility of the researcher to make new knowledge—though the call for originality is often tempered. As Greever and Jones' *Century Collegiate Handbook* (1939) put it, "A term paper . . . need not (except in advanced or graduate work) be exhaustive or add to human knowledge, it should leave no important phase of the subject untouched. . . . It is to be a product (1) of your examination and comparison of a number of sources and (2) of your independent thinking on the evidence, the theories, and the issues" (313).

While the trend in textbooks in the thirties and forties was clearly to fence off the freshman research paper from other essays and place it in the German-influenced tradition of scholarship, a number of texts didn't bother at all with framing the broader purposes of the assignment. By the 1940s, the term paper had already begun to fossilize into a generic assignment, a type of school writing that had become so commonplace that some authors assumed it required no explanation of rhetorical purpose or context. Typical of this was the first edition of the enormously influential and immensely popular *Harbrace Handbook of English* (Hodges 1941). Though the book devoted nearly forty pages to "Library and Term Paper," it was completely silent about why students might be asked to write one in the first place. The *Harbrace Handbook* presented the purpose of the term paper as largely one of narrowing a topic in which the student has "proper interest," going to the library, and then finding out "what has been written about it" (376).

However, among 1940s' writing textbooks that *did* put the research paper in some rhetorical context, only a few still categorized it as a form of exposition, and even in those the language of the research ideal dominated the discussion of the assignment. Pence's *Craft of Writing* (1944), for example, describes the research paper as "formal exposition," but then describes it as "the kind of writing that scholars produce in all fields of human knowledge" (203). By the late forties, the research paper began to achieve its now familiar status, with its own chapter and separate treatment. Completely divorced from exposition, the research paper genre finally shed its purpose of appealing to a general audience, and began to fulfill its role as a specialized genre intended for an audience of imagined experts. The authors of *American College English* (Warfel et al. 1949), for example, in a separate chapter on the "Research Essay," explicitly describe the assignment as preparation for serious scholarship.

> Every member of a profession sooner or later may be called upon to prepare for publication a statement of his research or his achievements. The students' research reports, term papers, theses, or dissertations, are training in methods of work which will be useful in a professional career . . . A research essay gathers and interprets a set of facts for the benefit of a specialized group of readers . . . At its weakest, the student essay should be a new selection of facts which develop his central idea; at best, it should be the development of a *new idea* from facts already known, or a new interpretation of facts hitherto unknown or not recognized as pertinent to the idea. By presenting an original view of the subject in an individual manner, the research essay can bring new insight to an old problem. (553–4; emphasis added)

The emphasis on originality remains a strong strand in these textbooks, but it now goes far beyond Baldwin's "originality of compilation" to fully embrace the research ideal's emphasis on the contribution of new knowledge and *ideas*. Though in their commentary some textbook authors in the forties and fifties still tempered their expectations that undergraduates can do serious scholarship, the ideal is celebrated in almost all of them I examined, at least in those that weren't silent on the assignment's purpose. While Eric Steel, in *Readable Writing* (1950), observes that masters' students must produce a "de luxe model" research paper, and doctoral students a "super de luxe model" (206), undergraduates can still aspire to "original work fashioned from secondhand material." Skeptical students are then treated to this pep talk.

> But everything has been written up, you may remonstrate. Not so! New fields of knowledge are opening up daily. When such a new area becomes the object of curiosity, writers deal with it like sparrows a chunk of bread. Each bird breaks off a beakful and concentrates temporarily on that. Similarly, each writer devotes an article to a tiny aspect of the big subject. When a number of articles have appeared, along comes another investigator who sifts, combines, evaluates, and so produces a book. Your paper will stand a better chance of being original if you select a subject on which that first book has not yet been written. (209)

By the 1950s, the treatment of the research paper assignment in composition rhetorics and handbooks took on all the familiar features we see in textbooks today. In addition to the emphasis on originality, on the need to imitate serious scholarship, and on the practical value of library skills, fifties' textbooks featured now-standard apparatus on research methods and conventions, including an extensive discussion of note cards, note-taking methods (paraphrase, summary, quotation), lists of key library references, models of citation methods, warnings against plagiarism, and usually a sample research paper. The conventions of the academic paper—how it should be structured and cited, how sources should be evaluated, how to avoid plagiarism, what constitutes an acceptable thesis and tone—become a primary concern, normally constituting the bulk of the chapter. There are at least several explanations for this, all of which are significant developments in the aims and methods of research paper instruction.

First, the research paper's final break with its historical association with exposition represented a major rhetorical shift. No longer were students writing essays based on reading intended for non-experts like themselves. Maintaining "reader interest" in the topic, always a primary concern for the expository writer, gave way to much more practical concerns. As Hook and Ekstrom put it in their 1953 text *Guide to Composition*, since the research paper is primarily intended to "convey information,"

> . . . its style is usually rather impersonal and even formal. Amiable chitchat, extensive use of the pronoun I, and the serene informality which often characterizes other writings are seldom regarded as appropriate. . . . Not that such a paper should be dull—far from it. But its interest should come chiefly from the content, from the wealth of pertinent details and examples. Its major stylistic trait should be clarity. (232)[6]

The research paper, stripped of its connection to other forms of writing and invested with a specialized purpose of conveying information to a narrow audience, has fewer aesthetic or expressive qualities. Language that is a barrier to content is considered inappropriate, losing both its constitutive and aesthetic functions, as well as its visible relation to authorship; instead, according to Hook and Ekstrom, "its major stylistic trait should be clarity." If, then, the primary purpose of the research paper is to be a vehicle for transmission of (hopefully) "original" information to specialized readers who are presumably already familiar with the topic, then the method of presentation becomes paramount. Above all, it must be "efficient." Formal conventions—how to structure the paper, where to place the thesis, how to properly paraphrase and cite, how to adopt the appropriate tone—attempt to reproduce efficient means of transmitting information that is familiar to a particular audience. Quite naturally, then, textbooks began to lavish more and more attention on the formal qualities of the research paper, and less and less on the writer's own particular purposes in exploring the topic or her duty to establish its significance to readers who may be unconvinced of its relevance to their lives. Before long, the buzzard's feet were tied.

The textbook emphasis on formal conventions might have another origin as well. While the drumbeat for originality in the research essay persisted since the assignment first appeared in writing texts—and it continues today—the ideal that freshman researchers can actually make an original contribution to knowledge cannot be taken seriously. No instructor really expects her students to be genuine scholars, the enthusiasm of some textbook writers, like Eric Steel, notwithstanding. That ideal became even more specious in the forties, fifties, and sixties, as disciplinary knowledge exploded and more fences went up on the commons. Lacking a way to evaluate their students' success in writing an "original" research paper—and privately believing that freshmen couldn't do it anyway—instructors embraced the proper use of conventions as a viable alternative. "Did they do it right?" rather than "What did they say that was original?" became the more convenient means of judging students' mastery of research writing.

Finally, the "service function" of freshman English—and in particular the obligation to teach the term paper for other departments—became a much more explicit purpose of the assignment by the 1950s, and the emphasis on research "skills"—especially the handling of formal conventions—increased as a goal of instruction. "Actually, you are introduced to research writing in your basic writing course because you will later need detailed instruction in it," wrote the authors of the 1957 text *Writing: A Functional Approach to College Composition*. The freshman English teacher "can more reasonably be expected to supply such instruction than could any of your other instructors. He will see you through the various steps in the writing of a practice paper" (232). These sentiments, though open to question (*why* is the composition instructor better suited to teaching research skills?), were widely shared by textbook authors, and of course continue to have great currency among current instructors as well. Training in the term paper, and in particular its conventions, became for many faculty outside the English department Freshman Composition's most obvious and valuable raison d'etre, and writing texts quickly responded to their demands.

The I-Search and Other Aberrations

By the 1960s, treatment of the assignment was fairly uniform among composition texts, but the competitive nature of the textbook market and continuing dissatisfaction with student papers produced a new approach. The "controlled research paper"—one written using sources included in a published topical collection—became increasingly popular in the sixties. Virtually every major textbook publisher began to produce slim volumes on a variety of single subjects, ranging from Salem witchcraft to Robert Frost, each featuring selected articles, reviews, criticism, and primary works. One of these controlled research texts would then be used by the entire class as a source material for a research paper. The library became superfluous. For example, Greenburg and Hepburn's *Robert Frost: An Introduction* (1961) was a controlled research text that featured progressively more difficult materials on the poet, and an extensive appendix listing "Topics for Papers." Short paper topics ask students to compare two critics who are included in the volume. Topics for longer research papers demand that students synthesize and analyze more material in the text. (For example, "Distinguish the different views of the critics on Frost's relationship to society. Make a case from the poems in the pamphlet for one that seems to you most satisfactory.") (175).

In an interview, Richard Larson recalled that when he entered the composition field in the early sixties, controlled research papers were all the rage. "The student would do the so-called research work except the student wouldn't do any research work since the research had already been done for him," Larson said. "This was a way, I suppose, to keep librarians from being inundated by students working on research papers for different courses. . . . It's all packaged, all you have to do is take the appropriate items out of the package and assemble them." Larson's analogy seems apt. The controlled research paper was an attempt to manage the process of research, and therefore help ensure a more uniform product. It allowed writing teachers to not only define the research topic—presumably something *they* were interested in and knew something about—but also supply students with suitable materials. The product orientation of the controlled research text seems perfectly consistent with current–traditional rhetoric, the dominant pedagogy at the time. But it was bound to fall out of favor with the rise of writing process pedagogies.

A leader of the writing process movement, Ken Macrorie published *Searching Writing* (in a later edition, *The I-Search Paper*) in 1980; the text was a radical response to research papers that Macrorie called "bad jokes." With sarcastic punch, he wrote that college research papers are "funny because they pretend to be so much and actually are so little" (161). His text (he actually termed it a *context*book) encouraged students to research topics that have immediate relevance to their lives (for example, buying a camera, exploring architecture as a profession) and tell the story of their search, or "quest." He strongly emphasized nonlibrary sources, especially interviews, and peer group

response. Macrorie's text quickly gained a small, but devoted following, particularly among high school teachers, and it remains the most
prominent alternative text on the research assignment.[7]

The novelty of the *I-Search Paper*, and Macrorie's public ridicule of
the traditional term paper were—and remain—isolated acts of resistance. By and large, the research paper chapter is still a fixture in contemporary rhetorics and handbooks. These chapters mostly *look*
remarkably similar to those in texts published thirty years ago. There
are some changes, however, inspired in part by the emphasis on writing process and developments in composition theory.[8] But these are
hardly major reforms. There is an effort, for example, among several
of the current texts I examined to expand the notion of research to
include investigations outside of the library, such as field research, interviews, and surveys. In fact, several new textbooks, including Elizabeth Chiseri-Strater and Bonnie Sunstein's *Fieldworking* (1997),
engage students exclusively in ethnographic research.

A number of contemporary textbooks frame the research paper in
terms of social theories of writing.[9] Of the books I examined, Charles
Bazerman's *The Informed Writer* (1992) does so most explicitly, beginning with the line "Although a writer may work in private, a writer is
never alone" (3). A researcher should cite sources, he adds in a later
chapter, because "you let the reader know the full extent of the conversation in which you are taking part" (322). A few authors—by no
means most—also take pains to suggest that research is not an activity separate from other kinds of writing as well. "[A]lmost all writing
involves research," writes Douglas Hunt in *The Riverside Guide to Writing*. "Rather than treating 'the research paper' as a separate type of
assignment, this chapter will suggest techniques useful for short papers and long 'personal' essays and formal term papers" (418).

While these departures from the conventional treatment of the
assignment are worth noting, in many more ways the representation
of the research paper in current composition textbooks reveals how
the genre remains captive to its history. Matthew Wilson concludes
that the "pervasive and fundamental assumption" in current texts'
treatment of the research paper is "positivist—that the work a student
does in writing a research paper is like the work of a scientist." It is an
assumption, Wilson argues, that "denies uncertainty and ambiguity
and which completely excludes the act of writing from the discussion"
(243). The extent to which the genre is still captive to the scientific
paradigm is also evident in the continuing emphasis in most texts on
ambiguous notions of originality, the nearly exclusive emphasis on
argument, the repudiation of subjectivity, and the near obsession with
the minutiae of research conventions.[10] As a rule, contemporary textbooks have very little to say about the aims of academic research, the

nature of inquiry, the students' role as knowers, or the importance of pursuing investigations that have personal or social significance. Nor do they have much to say about writing as a method of discovery *during* the research process.

More than anything else, chapters on the research paper reflect the continuing obligation writing instructors feel to indoctrinate students in research *skills* as a service to other departments; in these texts, the freshman research paper is seen as the primary vehicle for initiating students in the professional culture of the academy. The result is that the genre is still presented as unconnected to the other writing that is going on in the course, and the *essayistic* possibilities of fact-based writing—the promise that through writing one can explore not just what is known, but what it means to be a knower—are often completely ignored. In short, the research paper remains a genre that is viewed as largely untouchable by English teachers, existing outside of rhetorical and literary traditions. It belongs to someone else, yet we find ourselves stuck with it. Can we reclaim it in some way? Can we make it our own without totally sacrificing our obligations to introduce students to the practices of academic research?

Apathy, Atrophy, and the Freshman Research Paper

Though it now seems hard to imagine, there was a time when American college students didn't write term papers. It was a time when the well-spoken word was the measure of learning rather than the well-written one. It was a time when colleges students and their teachers were generalists rather than specialists, and discourse was polite, civil, and public—a matter of good taste, good rhetorical sense, and good memory. The research paper had no place in the "old college," but it was to assume a central role in the new one.

The transformation of the American university—from the small, homogenous college of antebellum period, to the beginnings of the modern university in the late nineteenth century—has been well documented by Veysey, Berlin, Kitzhaber, Russell, Veblen, Graff, and others. The growth of enrollments after the Civil War, and increased public disenchantment with the irrelevance and impracticality of the traditional "liberal education," with its single curriculum and emphasis on instilling the virtues of Christian values and mental discipline, gave way to the professionalization of the university. From 1865 to 1890, the notion of the American college was reformed to three more "specific conceptions," according to Laurence Veysey: "the aim of practical service, . . . the goal of abstract research, and . . . the attempt to diffuse standards of cultivated taste" (12). This transformation also implied a basic change in pedagogy. Because the mission of the old college was to train a new cultural elite for leadership in the church, in law, and in politics, it emphasized training in oratory.[11] And the belief that "mental discipline" could be achieved through drills and repetition led to particular kinds of oral performances, such as recitations and rhetoricals (Russell 36).

Several factors changed this, including the discrediting of the psychological theories that compared the mind with a muscle that could be strengthened by the "exercise" of recitation and drill (Kitzhaber 2). Another factor was the waning influence of the clergy in American colleges. But perhaps most important was the growing influence of German models of higher education, particularly their emphasis on scholarship that is text-based rather than oral. Along with this was a fundamental epistemological shift. In the old college, students were initiated in received truths, which were to be memorized, not questioned. In the modern university, truth was to be *discovered* through rigorous investigation. The central interest of the traditional college in the indoctrination of the *known*—the status quo—gave way to a passionate interest in exploring the *unknown*. American educators seized from the German model a new academic mission: to conduct original investigations that involved "rigorous and precise examination of phenomena, whether natural or historical" (Veysey 127).[12] Contributing to the growth of knowledge in an increasingly specialized field became the aim of the emerging "research ideal," and the means for reporting these discoveries was not the oral rhetorical but the documented "thesis" or "dissertation." According to Russell,

> The new text-based scholarship, along with the new differentiated
> academic structure, changed the nature of the academic game.
> Oral performance for a local academic community demanded only
> a *display* of learning, but the new text-based standards demanded
> an *original contribution* to a disciplinary community in written form:
> the research paper. The American scholarly journals, which
> developed in the late nineteenth century as a major forum for
> faculty discourse, contain a great deal more transcription of oral
> discourse (discussions, speeches, lectures) than do contemporary
> journals. But disciplines quickly evolved the text-based apparatus
> of modern scholarship: discipline-specific conventions of argu-
> ment, style, documentation, and format. (80; emphasis added)

As more and more faculty embraced the research ideal, the university, to accommodate this growth in specialized knowledge, became increasingly fragmented into separate departments, disciplines, and discourses. No longer were students exposed to a common curriculum; increasingly it became elective, and as it did, student writing "progressively moved away from the local academic community and into the individual classroom, the domain of specialized disciplinary knowledge" (Russell 80). Before long, faculty began to require graduate students, and later undergraduates, to imitate their own scholarly practices, including conducting original research and writing about it in properly documented term papers.

But how did the research paper end up in high schools? As the modern university emerged, it faced the problem of recruiting students who were prepared for its new research mission. Because the free public high school was largely nonexistent before the 1860s, many of the new state universities began their own college prep programs. In 1870, the University of Michigan pioneered another approach: certifying certain public high schools in the state as having "respectable collegiate preparation." This freed the colleges from their preparatory responsibility, allowing them to pursue the goals of the new scholarship, and according to Fredrick Rudolph, this "unleashed the high-school movement in the Middle West" as public educators saw the chance to elevate the standards of local schools (283). Soon other American colleges followed suit. In fact, some college administrators were so taken with the promise of high schools adopting a college curriculum that they began to entertain the idea that the new university might devote itself exclusively to the research ideal. According to Rudolph,

> the degree to which university ambition on the German model helped inspire the certification movement and the subsequent growth of high schools was revealed in an overly ambitious announcement of the University of Minnesota in 1871 that it intended as soon as possible to shift the work of its preparatory *and* collegiate departments to the high schools and eventually to limit the work of the university to professional study and graduate study in science, literature, and the arts. (283–4)

As college subjects were introduced into the high schools, the documented term paper obediently followed. And while the University of Minnesota's early vision of freedom from teaching undergraduates was clearly overambitious, the certification movement did succeed in enlisting high school teachers in the service of the research ideal and its new offspring: the documented research paper.

The Research Paper and the "Problems of Everyday Life"

It's not overstating the situation to say that the transformation of the American university was swift. "How rapidly had the aim of research achieved recognition?" asks Veysey.

Looking back, it is clear enough that in the 1870s research played no important role in American higher education. . . . Around 1880 a definite change occurred. It then began to be believed—whether rightly or not—that most of the "bright young men" were going into science. At just this time Harvard undergraduates began using the college library in significant numbers for research purposes. . . . [B]y 1910 research had almost fully gained the position of dominance it was to keep thereafter. (174–5, 177)

Ten years later, by the 1920s, the freshman research paper made its appearance in composition texts, reflecting many of the elements of the research ideal.[13] Student research papers should be "original," they should contribute to specialized knowledge, and they should be properly documented. While what constituted an "original contribution" to knowledge might have been clear in the nineteenth century when disciplines were beginning to form, the concept became more and more ambiguous to twentieth-century undergraduates and their instructors. The result, as David Russell put it, was a widening "intellectual gulf" between students and their instructors—each group instinctively recognizing that original research is an unrealizable ideal—and the "term paper gradually atrophied as a genre of student writing and gained a reputation as a hollow formal exercise" (87–8). Even today, as I've already observed, both writing teachers and students remain captive to a term that has become meaningless.

The essentially scientific conception of research adopted by American devotees of the German example, even for investigations in the humanities, has created further problems for the student writer of modern research papers. According to Patricia Sullivan, "science was the paradigm for all fields of inquiry," and its "epistemological assumptions" demanded "the researcher's detachment from . . . the ideas or phenomenon that comprised the objects of inquiry. Research was equated with objectivity and detachment . . ." (15). While arguably these notions of objectivity and detachment may be useful guidelines for a quantitative scientific investigation, few freshman undertake such projects in their composition classes. Students are inescapably *subjective* when they write on the causes of the Viet Nam War or how to battle bulimia. In fact, student researchers are often both subjective *and* objective: They must recognize their biases, yet attempt to measure those respectfully against other voices. Ironically, by admitting these biases, rather than pretending they don't exist, researchers can often adopt the stance that objectivity is intended to promote: a willingness to "hold personal judgments in check" (Charney et al. 570). But the scientific mandate of objectivity and detachment persists in term paper instruction, and the result is the widespread belief among students that they must not use "I," they should not express their "opinions," and they must not deploy personal experience in research papers.

The legacy of the research ideal has one other implication for the modern research paper, and it brings us back to Patricia Limerick's wired vultures and an academic culture that seems to have no relation to people's lives. The practices of the old college turned students and professors outward toward a larger academic community whose (often admittedly elitist) values they shared. But the practices of the modern university signaled a retreat into a more private, insular, and isolated way of being. Sullivan calls this the "myth of the independent scholar," the belief that research is essentially an asocial activity and that the production of knowledge is the act of an individual acting alone. Here's how Veysey put it:

> For the devotee of scientific investigation, Germany opened up the vista of a new goal, then dramatized by a process of initiation. The German laboratory and seminar offered these future American professors a novel mode of life, a private mode that turned them aside from the everyday world of society, politics, morality, and religion, even from the classroom itself, and removed them during most of their waking hours from their fellow men. (133)

As Sullivan notes, this conception denies the reality that most research is collaborative, but it also accounts for the problem raised in the beginning of this chapter. Academic researchers have, by and large, turned away from their fellow men and women, and they feel no particular obligation to make the written products of their research accessible. Perhaps ever since the research paper shed its association with exposition early in this century, students have essentially shared the belief that it is removed from the everyday world. Its subject matter, its language, and its presentation is, in their view, supposed to be formal, remote, and lifeless.

I believe the freshman research paper can—and should—renew its association with the everyday world. That involves reexamining the inherited assumptions that has kept the form captive. But it also means that composition stakes its own claim to the genre, and the rhetorical tradition's focus on public discourse represents a way to do that. In Hoyt Hudson's early and influential essay, "The Field of Rhetoric" (1923), he observes that the rhetorician is essentially a generalist, and that "rhetoric draws on other fields with considerable disregard for the airtight partitions sometimes put up between college departments." He writes,

> Aristotle, in discussing deliberative rhetoric, says that the subjects embraced are finance, war and peace, defence of country, imports and exports, and legislation. Yet the rhetorician does not necessar-

ily become an expert in those fields. He attempts to learn the authorities and sources of information in each, and to develop a method which he can apply to specific problems as they arise. He learns, in any given situation, what questions to ask—and to answer. The peculiar contribution of the rhetorician is the discovery and use, to the common good, of those things which move men to action—intangible, obscure, mystic, even as these things may be; yet you and I and our communities find them intertwined with every problem in life. (23)

Hunt offers the possibility of reconceiving the freshman researcher as a rhetorician rather than as a scientific investigator, and the research paper as a means of exploring how its topic is "intertwined with every problem in life." A new mandate—the need to discover how knowledge can be used to address specific problems that concern the common good—might replace the historical imperative that freshman researchers make original contributions to specialized knowledge. It is the loss of this rhetorical tradition—one that "gives primary emphasis to communication on public problems" (94)—that S. Michael Halloran mourns in his essay "Rhetoric in American College Curriculum." He writes that "the revival of rhetoric in the field of English composition has thus far failed to address the need for a revival of public discourse" (94). The freshman research paper, if it were to shed some the historical constraints imposed on it, seems the perfect vehicle for such a revival. It can do this without sacrificing its usefulness to other departments. Students will still receive training in documentation and methods of research, including library skills, and will practice certain habits of mind that encourage open inquiry. But even more important, students will see research as it should be seen: as an activity that need not shut out the nonspecialist, and one that can have a relationship to people's lives, including their own.

Notes

1. "Literature of Fact" is the title of a course that has been taught for some time at Princeton University by John McPhee, the nonfiction writer whose work exemplifies literary journalism.

2. The three-page survey was administered to students in nine randomly selected sections of our Freshman English course. A total of 196 students were surveyed, which represents 19 percent of the total population, and a degree of confidence of ±6 percent. Instructors of these nine sections also were surveyed by using an instrument nearly identical to the one administered to the students. The return rate on the instructor surveys was 100 percent, and the nine responses represent 20 percent of the total population (forty-five) of Freshman English instructors for the spring semester, 1995.

3. Though the results in Table 1–1 seem to largely reflect beliefs about the research paper that might arise from conventional instruction, there were some notable exceptions. For example, 55 percent of the respondents agreed that they could use their own experiences and observations as evidence in their papers, and only 36 percent agreed that "summarizing what's known about the topic is most important." Both are views that are somewhat at odds with the traditional emphasis on the researcher's detachment from her subject, the use of "authoritative" evidence, and the need to survey and report on current knowledge of a topic.

4. While source-based writing in the terms I describe it here—using material from the library, field observations, or interviews—to compose a research paper is a twentieth-century phenomenon, students of rhetoric have been composing source-based themes for centuries. The use of external sources, especially information from commonplace books, well-known historical narratives, and quotes from ancient authorities, was frequently called on to compose a theme that addressed an often abstract topic. One thing that most distinguishes this method of rhetorical invention from modern research is that it is meant to display already existing knowledge, not create new knowledge (for more, see Robert Connors, *Composition-Rhetoric*, pages 296–327).

5. Though my survey results suggest that freshmen who have written two or more term papers during their first year do not have different assumptions about the assignment than those who are writing their first paper for Freshman English, there is one exception: More experienced writers are even more likely to assume that their research papers should "say something original."

6. The sample research paper in this text—an essay titled "The Westinghouse Time Capsule," which explains the company's plan to use metallic alloys to build a time capsule that will last five thousand years—is at least stylistically everything its authors encourage, except that it *is* remarkably dull.

7. I greatly appreciate Macrorie's approach, and I recommend it as one of the best ways to teach students that curiosity is the best reason to research something. I find, however, that *I-Search* papers are not very interesting to read, though they're certainly more interesting than most formal research papers I've encountered.

8. I surveyed seven popular rhetorics and handbooks, in editions published in 1990 or later. They included *The Riverside Guide to Writing, Writing with a Purpose, The Informed Writer, The Bedford Handbook, The St. Martin's Handbook, The St. Martin's Guide to Writing,* and *The Random House Handbook.* I also examined James Lester's *Writing Research Papers,* for years the runaway best seller among specialized texts on the assignment.

9. Remarkably few of the popular composition texts highlight the social construction of knowledge, much less collaborative pedagogies, when discussing the aims and methods of the research paper. I remain amazed that more social theorists haven't seized this assignment as an opportunity to introduce students to ideas of the construction of knowledge.

10. An analysis of the model student research papers included in current writing texts is quite telling. All of the books I examined (even those like *The*

Riverside Guide, which attempted to recast the assignment) featured sample papers that excluded use of the first person and any use of the writer's experience or observations as evidence. Topics were never autobiographical, and all relied on argument. None seemed particularly original in any way, nor did the textbook's authors ever make claims about the originality of the student papers. Many of these papers, while competently written and organized and meticulously documented, were particularly uninspiring to read.

11. Writing was also a part of a student's experience in the American college during the antebellum period. Students might be asked to first write the theme that they will later recite, and grammar was often rigorously taught. Students were also expected to take lecture and lab notes (Brereton 4).

12. Veysey argues that U.S. professors might have taken the research mission much more seriously than did their German counterparts, especially the American devotion to scientific investigation. Paul Bernard and James Turner observe, in fact, that the American Ph.D. always required much more "substantial research" than did their counterparts in Germany.

13. How quickly did the "research ideal," which was initially emphasized at the graduate level, trickle down to undergraduate education? Russell claims it was more or less immediate, though at first rigorous "course theses" were viewed by some faculty as appropriate only for the most advanced students. Others had a more egalitarian position, arguing that all students, even those in secondary school, should write research papers, sometimes assigning a moral value to such a "personal discipleship in learning" (Russell 86). The elitist and egalitarian views towards undergraduate research created a long-standing "tension," says Russell, which college instructors never overcame: "[T]hey merely developed ways of living with it, ways that marginalized writing instruction" (87).

Two

Facing Facts
Knowledge, Identity,
and the Student Researcher

"Doing a research paper is like an atheist going to church on Sunday"
—A college freshman

When Becky Hodgkins was assigned a research paper in her high school English class, her instructor gave Becky photocopies of several chapters from the *MLA Handbook*—one on citation methods, another on compiling a bibliography, a third on format, and a fourth chapter that, in fairly typical fashion, described the aims of the assignment. The research paper should "present information and ideas clearly and effectively," intoned the *Handbook*, yet students should avoid becoming so "preoccupied" with the mechanics of gathering and documenting information that they "forget to apply the knowledge and skills they have acquired through previous writing experiences" (Gibaldi and Achtert 1). While the research paper may be similar to "other forms of writing," the *Handbook* continued, "it differs from many of them in relying on sources of information other than the writer's personal knowledge and experience." The emphasis of academic research is not on the arrangement of "other people's thoughts," but the "facts and opinions you draw from your research" (Gibaldi and Achtert 2).

Becky's topic was "Diabetes: Diagnosis, Complications, Treatments and Research," and from my point of view—and from hers—the resulting paper is a case study of what's wrong with conventional research paper instruction. Despite the *MLA Handbook*'s call to build the paper around the "opinions" the writer "draws" from her investigation, Becky has almost no presence in her paper at all, and when she does appear, however tentatively, the move draws criticism from her teacher. After three pages of factual summary on the definition, types, and identification of diabetes, there is finally an isolated attempt at "authorial intrusion":

> Most cases of adult-type diabetes can be controlled by a diet that is low in calories. Some adult-type diabetics whose condition cannot be controlled by diet alone use insulin or take oral drugs that reduce the level of sugar in the blood.
> Fads come and go. Hemlines of fashionable clothes go up and down from one year to the next. Science and medicine have had their own fads and fashions, and the treatment of diabetes is no exception.
> Before Banting and Best isolated insulin . . .

Becky's analogy between trends in fashion and trends in medicine moves tentatively towards interpretation—diabetes treatment is trendy like everything else—and towards more original language—note how she begins with a short, emphatic sentence that is a clear break with the prose of the preceding and following paragraphs. It was a move that elicited a single marginal comment by her teacher: "transition needed." The rest of Becky's paper retreats back into a report, all handled quite competently if lifelessly; that is, until the final concluding paragraph. Here the writer returns and once again she explicitly registers her presence:

> Diabetes is the fourth leading cause of death from disease; it is a silent killer affecting fourteen million Americans. At least 65,000 people in Maine. Even more frightening is the fact that more than half of the people with diabetes do not know they have this serious disease.
> There are really only two ways to approach life, as a victim or as a gallant fighter, and you must decide if you want to act or react, deal your own cards or play with a stacked deck. And if you don't decide which way to play with life, it always plays with you.

While at first Becky's ending seems an abrupt shift in tone and treatment (her instructor circled all the *you*'s and edited the contraction *don't* to *do not*), I began to read the ending of her essay as a desperate justification of the entire paper, and perhaps the entire genre of the "objective" research report. If the assignment were essentially to collect and report on information that was widely available elsewhere—without comment or interpretation by the writer and without a real audience or purpose—then the value of such an exercise must reside in the belief that knowledge itself has power, that its mere existence—even on display in the pages of a term paper—helps you "deal your own cards" and "play with life" rather than be victimized by it.

Becky had to know that her paper would likely never be read by diabetics, including the great numbers of people who "do not even know they have the disease." Nor does the paper contribute anything that is new about the illness. So what gives this assignment meaning? If it doesn't move a reader to act or contribute new knowledge to the field, does it at least change the writer? It doesn't seem to. There is no evidence that Becky's paper invited her to assume a new role as a researcher, as a knower, as someone with something to say about diabetes—not until the end of the paper, that is, where Becky seems to declare not only that diabetics and others can take control of their lives with knowledge, but that her effort to collect that knowledge might be worthwhile. In the margin next to that final paragraph, Becky's instructor wrote simply, "a more-extensive, more formally-worded conclusion is needed."

What *really* seems to be behind this assignment is simple: Can the students follow the rules? Despite the photocopied instructions admonishing students to avoid becoming preoccupied with the mechanics of research, nearly all of the instructor's written comments focused on problems with conventions, including improper placement of material on the title page (paper title, author's name, and date were placed two inches too high), inappropriate use of "informal" language (for example, use of the pronoun *you* to address readers), weak transitions, and improperly titled outline and appendices. The instructor's preoccupation with the technical conventions of research is most evident in a "Mechanical Abstract," a worksheet he gave to his students. In it they are asked to check off when they have completed each part of the paper (title page, rationale, proposal, abstract, outline, text, etc.), as well as quantify and list not only the number and types of sources students consulted, but how many times they are cited in the text. Becky, he claimed, had miscounted. Note cards were to be color-coded by type of source (blue for magazines, green for books, orange for pamphlets, etc.), punched with a single hole in the upper right-hand corner, and bound by a metal ring.

This level of compulsiveness about the mechanics of writing the research paper may be extreme, but I don't think it's atypical, particularly in high school instruction. If college instructors quietly despair at fulfilling the historical injunctions to encourage originality and independent thinking in student research papers, then many high school teachers must feel positively hopeless about it. A focus on whether students handle conventions correctly, rather than whether they have "original" things to say, is perceived as a much more realistic way to evaluate students' success at research writing. High school English teachers are also bound by their own notions of service—to prepare college-bound students for academic writing—and ever since the term paper became a fixture in undergraduate courses, secondary instructors have dutifully taught their juniors and seniors The College Research Paper.[1] It is normally a very conventional conception of the genre, with all the inherited (and mostly scientific) assumptions about it mentioned in the last chapter.

Though it would be easy—and part of an unfortunately long tradition—to blame ill-informed high school teachers for frustration with the research writing of college freshmen, secondary English instructors are in the same position as their college counterparts: "stuck" with teaching a specialized writing genre for someone else, and operating under inherited beliefs—mostly uncritically accepted—about what a research paper must be. My own experience working with high school teachers on research paper instruction suggests that they also share similar frustrations with the assignment. Unfortunately, there has been essentially no dialogue between college and high school teachers about how to prepare students for academic research. It's a situation that prompted one of my former students, after I told her of proposed changes in the ways research is taught in college composition, to say with exasperation, "I think you guys and the high school teachers should get together and talk. I suppose if change happens, it happens from the top down, not the bottom up. By the time high school teachers get wind of what's going to happen, you're going to be changing again" (Boncek).

The fact remains, however, that the attitudes students bring to Freshman English towards the research paper are profoundly shaped by their first contact with the genre in high school. The data from the survey discussed in the last chapter—as well as my own experience with secondary teachers—suggest that the dominant research paper pedagogy in high school reflects the familiar scientific paradigm, including many elements of the "research ideal": an emphasis on originality, objectivity, detachment, and topics removed from the "everyday world." The audience of the high school research paper is usually assumed to be limited—usually the teacher. By far, however, the greatest attention is paid to the formalities of research writing: citation, format conventions, and structure.

It shouldn't be any surprise, then, that when high school students walk into the college composition classroom their assumptions about the research assignment may disappoint their instructors and frustrate their efforts to get students to do something meaningful with the assignment. I believe that the attitudes of University of New Hampshire freshmen, mostly fresh out of high school, are typical.[2] When they were asked to check statements in a survey that reflected their assumptions about the research paper assignment, over half agreed that the first person should not be used in research papers (57 percent), books are a primary source of information (52 percent), they need to "follow a formal structure" (69 percent), one should have a thesis before the research begins (61 percent), and the researcher must be "objective" (60 percent). Only 22 percent believed that they were supposed to use their own opinions in a research paper. Several of these assumptions are troubling, and many are wrong. Researcher's opinions are central to academic inquiry. Much academic research relies on a range of data sources other than books, including field observations and case studies. While the use of first person is not the norm for reporting research, it is increasingly common in many fields, including the sciences. Notions of "objectivity" are increasingly under attack. And many researchers undertake research projects largely for the purpose of discovery—an idea that seems at odds with the assumption that one always begins with a thesis.

But even if some of these beliefs are arguably true, are they helpful to beginning researchers? Do they contribute to the idea that researchers are not just receivers of knowledge but makers of knowledge? If students construe "objectivity," the ban on the use of first person, and the exclusion of personal opinion in research writing as a mandate to remove any evidence of authorship from their papers, are they likely to understand research as a process in which they are involved in the negotiation about what might be true? Does the assumption that they must have a thesis at the beginning of the process subvert the idea of research as discovery? And does the apparently widespread belief among students that research writers must always follow a formal structure foreclose other possibilities and purposes for creating knowledge—accounting, for example, for how it was acquired, or sharing it with non-academic audiences? Seen more broadly, these questions hint at two larger concerns I'd like to take up in this chapter—to what extent do student writers of research papers see themselves as subjects of their research, and what kinds of roles do they construct for themselves as knowers?

Surrender of the Self: Caught in the Sterile Cage

For many students, writing a research paper, particularly after months of writing essays, presents a very practical problem: What happens to the self? My former student Jayne, coming off a remarkable performance in her personal essay "The Sterile Cage," seemed to fail miserably when faced with the research paper. Matthew Wilson argues that Jayne's problem may lie with a "certain incompatibility between writing that is overtly autobiographical and writing that demands students suppress the autobiographical, between expressive writing and writing that is assumed to be the antithesis of the expressive" (241). This shift from personal to research writing, Wilson believes, is an "impossible transition." Jayne was silenced in the research paper because the "world of solipsism" created by expressive writing did not prepare her to "connect those narratives to history, culture, or community," to other voices and ideas (251).[3]

I think there's a much simpler explanation. Jayne's failure had less to do with solipsism than the remarkable power of the inherited assumptions about the research paper genre. When confronted with the assignment, Jayne, like many students, shifted to a default program she was amazed I didn't acknowledge: "It's a research paper, goddammit, it's supposed to be this way!" After experiencing the subjectivity of the essay, students like Jayne are confronted with the historical injunction that in the research paper they should be detached, disinterested, and objective. At the same time, they are encouraged to be "original," a term that can be understood to mean a variety of things: an original contribution of ideas, an original presentation of existing material, the creation of new knowledge, or original expression. Several of these meanings are embedded in this fairly typical introduction to the research paper in Bazerman's *The Informed Writer:* "The research paper is an original essay presenting your ideas in response to information found in library sources. As you gather research material, your ever-increasing knowledge of a topic will allow you to make informed judgements and original interpretations" (269).

Confronted with the demand for "informed judgements" and "original interpretations," and the insistence they do more than simply report collected facts but invest them with their own novel ways of seeing and thinking, students frequently conclude that in this college research paper, at least, they are "supposed to use their opinions." But for many students, the injunction that they express their opinions in their research papers seems at odds with the imperative to avoid evidence of authorship. Rightly or wrongly, the perceived ban on use of the first person in research papers is, in the minds of many student writers, one of the guiding principles of objective writing. Unable to see how they can register their presence in a term paper without referring to themselves in some way, many freshman writers conclude that their opinion isn't really important after all. The practical result of this paradox is often crossed signals between instructors and students, typified by Becky's paper, where writers quickly learn that teachers don't mean what they say. Another consequence is that student writers are effectively silenced, trapped like Jayne was, in a sterile cage where the only sound is the voice of Authorities.

Is the emphasis on personal writing at least partly to blame for this silence, as Matthew Wilson suggests? Might Jayne have done better on her research paper if she had not been encouraged to write "The Sterile Cage" in the opening weeks of my course? Would she have been more able to "suppress the autobiographical" and seen other ways of registering her presence in her research paper? Possibly. But it seems even more likely to me that she would have simply accepted silence as a condition of academic writing. It is in the often difficult negotiation between the subjectivity of the essay and the supposed objectivity of the research paper that I now find students have the most to learn about inquiry. It is precisely *because* students have "tried on" being authors through personal writing that the move into research writing is so instructive, and so important. And often one of the first things they grapple with is their tacit theories of knowledge.

In the Way of Jennifer's Enlightenment

The other day I was talking to a student, now a senior, about when she felt competent as a writer of research papers. "I don't know," Jennifer said. "I think it was when I began to look at facts differently. I was always taught you don't question facts, you just summarize them." Jennifer describes, of course, a shift in the way she saw both knowledge and authority, something we certainly hope to teach in an introduction to research writing. But I fear we rarely do when the freshman research paper assignment embraces the scientific paradigm that is so pervasive in composition today, including the preoccupation with objectivity and originality, the nearly exclusive emphasis on argument, and the thesis–example structure. Much current research paper instruction is still rooted in positivist, arhetorical theories of knowing, which attempt to maintain a separation between the knower and the known and to view language as "merely a conduit for transmitting preexisting, preformed truth" (Russell 73). Writing is peripheral, useful only for getting things down on note cards and for reporting results. It does no real intellectual work. And when the emphasis in the research paper is always *to prove* rather than *to find out*, I worry that students will simply decide on a position and perform ritual hunting-and-gathering activities, never questioning facts, as Jennifer did, because they largely already agree with them.

In fact, many of our students seem already intellectually predisposed to do just that. Why is it that, despite our admonitions, in their research papers we want students to think independently, consider multiple perspectives, and incorporate their own judgments and interpretations, but they still resort to the familiar default program—merely parroting what experts say—or enact the other extreme—ignoring sources altogether and offering a paper full of their "opinions?" I've become more convinced that when we ask students to find their own purposes and use their own ideas in a research paper, they don't understand what we mean because our pedagogies fail to take into account their particular ways of knowing.

If we're teaching research correctly, we not only are taking the epistemological assumptions of our students into account, but also are looking for ways to get students to examine those assumptions. The intellectual development of college students and other adults is the subject of much work familiar to writing teachers, including works by William G. Perry, Mary Belenky et al., Nona Lyons and her colleague Carol Gilligan, Marlene Schommer, and more recently Charney, Newman, and Palmquist. Each of these studies offers different (sometimes competing) schemes for describing the epistemological patterns of college students and others.

Perry's is, by far, the most complicated (see Appendix A). It describes students' intellectual growth in four major, overlapping stages—simple dualism, complex dualism, relativism, and commitment in relativism—but then breaks these down into nine "positions," each further detailing the particular epistemologies of students at each position. While I find Perry's scheme quite helpful as a framework for describing students' struggles with knowledge and authority in the research paper, this study has been sharply criticized for, among other things, its gender and class bias. The subjects of his investigation were almost exclusively male students at Harvard and Radcliffe.[4]

Belenky and her colleagues' *Women's Ways of Knowing* offers an alternative account of adult intellectual development. The authors observe that their study "focuses on what else women might have to say about the development of their minds and on alternative routes that are sketchy or missing in Perry's version" (9). Like Perry, the Belenky investigation is based on interviews (in this case, with 135 women), but it describes the epistemological categories that resulted as *perspectives* rather than stages. Its authors are careful to avoid suggesting, as critics charge Perry does, that their subjects' development is linear. The five perspectives that emerged from the study of Belenky et al.—silence, received knowledge, subjective knowledge, procedural knowledge, and constructed knowledge (see Appendix A)—describe women's experience of knowledge and authority as ranging from feeling "voiceless" and at "the whims of external authority," to seeing that they are capable of reproducing and finally constructing knowledge, including a familiarity with the methods of "obtaining and communicating" it (15).

Recent work by Charney, Newman, and Palmquist further complicates Perry's stage model—and perhaps implicates much other developmental theory—by suggesting that it is too simplistic. They argue that students do not fit neatly into linear, easily categorized "epistemological styles," but rather exhibit ways of knowing that often mix "in varying concentrations," even though they may be inconsistent or even contradictory. Newman offers a much more condensed version of Perry's constructs—absolutism, relativism, and evaluatism—and finds that a student can, for example, be an absolutist *and* a relativist depending on the topic or the context (Charney, Newman, and Palmquist 7). Schommer, along with Jehng, Johnson, and Anderson agree, arguing that students' epistemological beliefs are "multi-dimensional," involving clusters of independent beliefs about the nature of learning as well as the nature of knowledge, rather than the "one-dimensional" beliefs Perry seems to suggest (Schommer 498; Jehng, Johnson, and Anderson 32).

These are significant criticisms, but I don't think they seriously undermine the value of Perry's work. The claim that student epistemologies are multidimensional is a sensible one, but the thoroughness of Perry's study, limited as it might be, still makes it enormously useful. However, I find that the characterization of Perry's work as linear is vulnerable to the same charge leveled at him—it oversimplifies. While he clearly does suggest that many of his students *progress* intellectually and morally, he also describes their development as wavelike rather than linear, involving both forward movement and regression. Perry observes that his students also, at times, held contradictory epistemological beliefs. Nonetheless, these criticisms of the "stage model" approach of describing students' intellectual development suggest that any categorical claims about where students are *developmentally* must be qualified.

I want to argue here that the research paper is a troubled genre because it is caught in the crossfire between competing epistemological assumptions. Conventional research instruction, typified by Becky's high school experience, is largely rooted in Enlightenment notions of truth, knowledge, and perception. While these notions are largely discredited by contemporary scholarship, the persistence of conventional approaches to the research paper in college composition has contributed to its status an empty exercise. Worse, they reinforce many epistemological assumptions that run directly counter to our current thinking about the nature of knowledge. In other words, the formal research paper, inspired by the scientific paradigm, might have very well stood in the way of Jennifer's enlightenment.

Freeing the research paper from its tightly tethered attachment to the nineteenth-century research ideal will help, but it also must be reconceived to be more consistent with modern theories of knowledge, something I explore more fully in the next chapter. However, how we resurrect the research paper depends on something we've long ignored: the epistemological assumptions of our students. How to best introduce students to research in Freshman English depends on starting with where they are epistemologically. In the rest of this chapter, I attempt to identify—relying largely on the studies of Belenky et al. and Perry—some of our students' epistemologies and how they may complicate their performance as research writers. In particular, two student writers in a Freshman English program, Carrie and Michael, provide, I think, a revealing look at how ways of knowing guide their thinking about the research paper. I met with each student five times as they worked on the assignment in the last six weeks of classes and transcribed roughly three hours of interviews with each.

Of course, the epistemologies of our students are not static. Much college instruction, and the research paper assignment in particular, hope to challenge their beliefs, to move students to more sophisticated notions about the nature of knowledge. We especially hope they will see that they can participate in knowledge construction, that "there is room for many voices" (Penrose and Geisler 517), including theirs. Sadly, conventional research paper instruction has essentially squandered the opportunity to give students a sense of themselves as knowers. By perpetuating the myth of objectivity and focusing largely on procedural knowledge rather than personal knowledge, traditional pedagogies eliminate the dissonance that challenges our students to reexamine their beliefs. That dissonance is not about procedure, but identity. And it's only when we encourage composition students to "get personal" in their research projects that they're likely to see themselves and their relationship to knowledge in a new way.

What Michael Said: Confessions of the Epistemologically Challenged

In our last interview session, Michael, one of the students I had been following as he worked on a research project, grew quiet and thoughtful. I had grown to admire him in the five weeks we'd talked. Though only eighteen years old, Michael seemed to welcome the opportunity to reflect on what he'd learned experimenting with his approach to research that semester, and at times seemed wise beyond his years. Still, he startled me when, after I pressed him on how he would distinguish between a *fact*, an *opinion*, and an *idea*, he suddenly said, "The word *fact* is a dangerous word."

"In what way?" I said.

"Well, Newtonian physics. They said that the Bohr model of the atom, the nice planar atom, was a factual description and everybody said, yeah, that's good. Until they started looking at them, at which point everybody realized the fact was wrong."

"He could be quoting Thomas Kuhn," I thought. I wondered what it might mean to understand this at the age of eighteen, so I asked him, "Michael, what about truth? What is your perspective on truth these days?" While that seems an abstract, airy question to ask, it was something we had talked about before in quite specific terms. As Michael researched his essay on the impact of sex and violence on television, I frequently prodded him to tell me how he determined which of his sources to believe, especially when they were in conflict. His answer to that question had evolved, and I sensed that he had arrived at some more personal understanding, one I hadn't, frankly, expected, despite his thoughtfulness.

"I don't have the vaguest idea," he said, "which makes being a Catholic extremely difficult. I find myself reaching closer and closer to a true neutral . . . [and] someone who is truly neutral will never do anything. They'd sit there weighing the possibilities of standing up and sitting down . . . I find myself getting closer and closer to that."

"Sounds like paralysis," I said.

"Almost. But a mental paralysis. I have beliefs that I'd like to follow through with, but at the same time, the more and more information I get, the more everything starts coming to a balance, . . . and who's to say what is right?"

"Is that a weird place to be in?"

"Yes, especially at eighteen years of age. Not having any clue what's right or wrong is very, very odd. I'm not sure exactly how it's going to pan out for my life yet."

I wondered, too. But must admit I delighted in Michael's confusion. As I listened to him work through the idea that truth is a contestable claim—which makes all "facts" suddenly suspect—and confront what this implies about "following through" with his own beliefs, it occurred to me that this confusion is exactly what the research assignment ought to invoke. Suddenly, usually abstract questions about the nature of knowledge became profoundly personal: "I'm not sure how it's going to pan out for my life yet." Michael's emotional, even uncomfortable response, according to William Perry, reflects the "revolution in identity" (114) that often accompanies intellectual growth, a transformation that can call into question what students believe about themselves, and alter their relationships with those structures that sustained their previous beliefs, including their family, their churches or synagogues, and their former teachers and schools. As Perry observes, "The conscious question 'Is *every*thing relative?' can lead (the student) to question 'Even me? My own values? My own certainties?'" (115). This potentially makes the freshman research paper anything but the exercise in objectivity and disinterestedness implied by traditional ped-agogies. It is deeply *subjective*. The real subject of a student's research paper, then, may not be the three best treatments for diabetes, or the impact of sex and violence on television, but his struggle to forge a new identity for himself as a knower. But how do students like Michael come to see that research can have such personal stakes?

On Opinions and Feelings

In addition to learning how to do laundry, open a checking account, and reverse telephone charges, two of the great revelations of the first year of college are not only that one can have an opinion, but also that it can have value. I am always struck by this when I assign the fresh-man research paper. I explain that this paper may be different from the ones they wrote in high school; rather than reporting what's known about their topics, students are expected to use the ideas of others to explore ideas of their own.

"You mean I can use 'I'?" they say.

"Certainly," I say.

"And I can put my own opinions in?"

"That's the idea."

If Becky's experience with the high school research paper is typical, then my students' reaction to being encouraged to express themselves in research-based writing shouldn't be surprising. "I just think a research paper is strictly facts," said Carrie, a second semester freshman, during one of our interviews about her research project in Freshman English. "I think of it as going to the library, going every way, and getting straight facts and just writing it that way. Just describing it, giving total informa-tion without getting the writer's two cents or anything into it."

Unlike many students, when Carrie is given the license, she has no difficulty expressing her "opinion." Despite the warnings against using the first person in high school papers, and her belief that most "formal" research papers assign no cash value to the writer's opinions, Carrie cannot imagine writing a paper in which she doesn't register her views. "I'm not a formal person," she observes. "I think even when I write formal, my opinion still comes through in my essay."

Abstractions about the nature of knowledge obviously have little power for students like Carrie. For them, an initial struggle with forming an identity for themselves as knowers seems to center on the meaning and value they place on their *opinions*. It is a word I heard often in my discussion with students about their research, and it carries heavy freight.

It's hard to imagine that students may claim to have no opinions, regardless of whether they are permitted to express them in term papers. But Perry's study, and especially Belenky and her colleagues' *Women's Ways of Knowing*, suggest that students who are "basic dualists," and women whose perspective is "silenced," are both likely to view all sources of knowledge as outside the self. For Perry's simple dualist, absolute Truth exists within unquestioned Authority figures. Personal opinion is completely subordinated to a faith in the certainty of others in a better position to know. The silenced women of Belenky et al.'s study share a similar view towards all-knowing Authority, but for many of these subjects, gender stereotypes reinforce their denial of self-knowledge: "Thinking for themselves violates their conceptions of what is proper for a woman," writes Belenky and her co-authors. "Another woman said, 'I didn't think I had a right to think. That probably goes back to my folks. When my father yelled, everybody automatically jumped. Every woman I ever saw, then, the man barked and the woman jumped. I just thought that women were no good and had to be told everything to do'" (30–1).

While few freshman entering college are basic dualists (Perry's Position 1), he observes that dualism is a much more common epistemological view in early adolescence, which may in part explain why the "paste pot and shears" method of the high school research report strikes some students as the only sensible way of approaching the assignment. The observation of Belenky et al. that perceived gender roles complicate silenced women's epistemological perspectives seems especially relevant for college instruction. While I have rarely encountered women in freshman English who fit this description of *silenced*—submissive, socially isolated, feeling both "deaf and dumb," and unable to see past the immediate, limited present—the authors' conclusions suggest that women especially might have more difficulty publicly committing to an opinion, and at the very least have a more complicated relationship with male Authority. How might this play out in a research paper?

Among other things, the work of Belenky et al. points to the particular difficulty our female students might face when developing a sense of themselves as knowers, and as a result, women may find the freshman research paper assignment especially challenging. Women who are silenced would likely find the demand for "originality" and independent thinking incomprehensible. On the other hand, these women would likely welcome the injunction to be objective, to extract the self from the discourse. Why not turn the discourse over to all-knowing Authorities? Conventional approaches to teaching the research paper might be particularly unproductive for women who already feel "deaf and dumb."

Carrie, like most college students I've encountered, is by no means silenced: "I think adding opinions is easier for me. I think that if I had to write a paper and I couldn't put my opinion in it at all, I would have a lot of trouble. . . . I think my brain works in opinion mode." Nor is she a simple dualist. While she is willing to grant an authority the benefit of the doubt—"You would figure that he's . . . done a lot more research"—Carrie is quite willing, in many cases, to see her opinion as equally valid.

> I think that's why I like to use my opinion in papers because I put my opinion along with what the author feels . . . even if it's against it. The author says this, but through my own research or whatever, I've found . . .[5]

One reason for Carrie's unwillingness to grant authorities the exclusive access to the Truth so characteristic of the dualistic thinker is her belief that "no one's opinion is wrong."

> That's one thing that I've always felt really strong about. I don't think anybody's opinion is wrong. When I was growing up in the CCD and stuff . . . I was killed and smashed for my opinions and I was going to hell for it, and it's one thing I've always been really strong about—that an opinion is an opinion. It's not a fact. It's something that someone feels. No one can tell you that your opinion is wrong. Because who is to say that their opinion is right? I don't think there really is right or wrong. I think you can think someone's opinion is right or wrong, but I don't think it can be definitely right or wrong.

Perry concludes that most second-semester college freshmen occupy Position 4 in his scheme. In Position 3, Perry's students begin to recognize a persistent—but they suppose temporary—level of uncertainty, even in some scientific fields, which up until then had seemed immune to it. After exposure to multiple perspectives in their high school and college courses, these students begin to recognize that there may not be wide agreement among experts. They shift from dualism to what Perry calls "multiplicity." What had seemed like temporary ambiguity about what is True is now seen as a relatively permanent condition of knowledge. These students are on the verge of embracing relativism, a step that Perry characterizes as a "revolutionary restructuring" of their thinking.

One student response to this recognition that Authorities don't always know, according to Perry, is the claim that since all knowledge is uncertain, who can say who is right? As Carrie put it, "No one can tell you your opinion is wrong," including the religious authorities who, in her past, wouldn't entertain dissent. There is, in this view, an element of active opposition—and in some cases, *reaction*—to authority. The study of Belenky et al. offers important insight into the origin of this opposition. Almost half of the 135 women she interviewed were what she called "subjective" knowers; it is a perspective roughly equivalent to Perry's Position 4 in its emphasis on the inherent validity of internal authority over external authority, but this valorization of self-knowledge originates not exclusively from educational experiences, as Perry suggests, but from personal ones. First-hand experiences with *"failed male authority,"* in particular, or some kind of devaluing of their personal ways of seeing seem crucial to their movement into subjectivism (57). For Carrie, it was, in part, her Catholic upbringing (and perhaps CCD—or catechism class—in particular), that reinforced her subjectivism, but she also alluded more vaguely to other experiences: "I've always known that my opinion has always been in papers, and that's because when I was younger I was always told that my opinion was not right, that I shouldn't have an opinion." As Carrie embraced her right to express her opinion, her relationship to authority shifted, too. While discussing the O.J. Simpson court case, Carrie assailed the tendency people have to grant certain people's opinions "superiority," or the right of certain people to assume their opinions are superior.

> There are certain people, I think we assume that their opinion is better than ours without really thinking about it. Obviously, Lance Ito, whatever he says, it's worth a lot more than whatever we would say. I think a lot of people are given that superiority . . . Why does he get to say? Because he's up there with a robe on?

Compare Carrie's response to authority—something she articulated at the beginning of her project—to the one implied by Michael's earlier comments, which he shared in our final interview. While Carrie saw external authority as a threat to her own beliefs and seemed to defend them by questioning the idea of authority itself, Michael made his beliefs vulnerable and open to challenge by others' versions of the truth.

Carrie also embraced a theory that I frequently hear from beginning researchers: There is a fundamental difference between *opinion* and *fact*. An opinion is *not* fact, Carrie was careful to point out. Opinions are "just something you feel" while, at least at the beginning of her research project, she viewed a fact as "something definite," particularly in science. According to Carrie, her research paper, which explored whether *The Simpsons*, an animated television show, had any redeeming social value, was a paper "more based on 'I thinks' than 'I knows,'" more on opinions than facts. It did not pretend to be author-itative, particularly in the scientific sense, as Carrie, who is a biology major, understood it.[6] What is crucial here is that, for Carrie, an *opinion* is a tentative statement of belief associated with *feeling*, not with thinking. Consequently, to deny the validity of an opinion, to argue against it, doesn't simply violate her sense of fairness, but strikes her as a personal attack.

As Belenky points out, this makes subjectivist women much less interested in persuading someone to share their point of view, some-thing that "can lead to unpleasant battles and threaten to disrupt rela-tionships" (70). As Carrie put it, "I'm not one to argue. I guess that's just the way I've been brought up. It's just, like, you express your opinion. I probably wouldn't sit there and argue with you. I would just know how I feel about it. For me, that's all that matters."

The Argument Against Argument

The nearly exclusive emphasis on argument—or as feminist critic Olivia Frey puts it, the "adversarial method"—as the mode of dis-course in conventional research papers would obviously create prob-lems for female students like Carrie. So would the assertion that, as the *MLA Handbook* asserts, the research paper should rely "on sources of information other than the writer's personal knowledge and expe-rience" (Gibaldi and Achert 2), for as Belenky et al. point out, person-al experience becomes a central source of knowledge for subjectivist women.[7] Invalidating personal knowledge restricts the ability of these students to "express their opinions" in research papers, since truth is often "grounded" in "first-hand experience" (Belenky et al. 61), and it robs them of a means of evaluating the truth of others' claims.

The belief that the researcher must be authoritative, that she must "come to definite conclusions" about her subject—an assumption that has it roots in the scientific paradigm that dominated the research ide-al[8]—further confounds students like Carrie who are much more ten-tative in their beliefs. They are much more comfortable with "I thinks" than "I knows"; the authoritative stance typical of argumentative dis-course implies a certainty they simply don't feel. When Carrie shared her research paper draft with a friend who had more formal high school instruction in research papers (Carrie had written very few in high school), the friend urged her to remove the "I thinks" in the pa-per and replace them with more conclusive statements.

> She actually liked [the paper] a lot. It's just that she wasn't sure
> how I was supposed to do it. . . . Like I had a couple "I thinks" and

she's, like, you're not supposed to think you're supposed to know! I'm, like, well it's my opinion! It's an "I think" [paper]. I changed to "I came to the conclusion to" . . . [in] a couple of [places].

Convinced by her reader that she is doing it "wrong," Carrie gave in on the stylistic convention that implies an authoritative claim, but it became obvious that this move was done half-heartedly. Carrie did not lack a commitment to her "opinion" here. Quite the contrary, like most relativists, she defended her opinions vigorously, particularly those she had developed on her own initiative or that grew out of her own experience. She was simply unwilling to imply the universality of her beliefs. Carrie was, however, willing to believe that she hadn't followed the "rules" of the research paper, and dutifully—though with little commitment—obeyed the injunction from some unseen authority that in a research paper one should *know*, not think.

Similarly, Carrie assumed that in formal research papers she must "pretend to be objective," something she admitted she is probably incapable of doing. "They want you to write it from the objective point of view. Standing back and just putting down all the facts." "Pretending to be objective," like faking certainty when one wants to leave room for doubt, is another of the masquerades a college researcher must play to do it "right."

Research and Responsibility

Carrie might easily conclude from this, as many students have, that in academic writing, one compromises honesty to follow someone else's script, or as one student put it, doing a research paper is "like an atheist going to church on Sunday." For these students, the coercive power of authority to force them to conform to arbitrary rules might deepen their unproductive resistance to authority—the position Carrie seemed to take when she wondered aloud whether Lance Ito's robe gives him an arbitrary edge—and lead to the alienation that Perry fears will undermine students' willingness to take responsibility for their opinions. This becomes a particular danger for students like Carrie, who, like many college freshman, are committed to relativism or subjectivism. As Perry observes,

> Relativism . . . if left at the level of conformity to Authority's demands can be exploited in gamesmanship: "I guessed it would be good to seem in favor of the book, but I didn't forget to be balanced." Here, then, the capacity to think about thought offers a position of detachment which can be exploited, as the sophists learned to exploit it, to evade responsibility. (108)

The emphasis on procedural knowledge at the expense of personal belief in conventional term paper instruction might also give academic research a mercenary quality: It doesn't matter what you believe just as long as you make a good argument.

Michael was keenly aware of the gamesmanship involved in the traditional research paper. He was more experienced with the genre than was Carrie: He wrote several high school research papers, and a formal critical paper for his college Shakespeare course last semester. For all of these papers Michael said he adopted a "dry, drab, impersonal, . . . pretty third-person" writing style. While he seemed to diminish that approach, unlike Carrie he understood it not as an arbitrary imposition by Authority, but as a rhetorical strategy.

> [Research papers] have to *look* objective. You may be shading the facts, or cutting off the right part of what an author said to make it come out the way you want it to, and say something that isn't necessarily straight out of the book. As long as everything looks kosher, everybody's happy. Obviously, you're pretty much coloring everything with your opinion anyway. . . . But everything should look like you're being very objective. . . . *Theoretically, you could get information to support any opinion you want.* It should be possible, and it's a matter of how well you weave that together to make your point more than anything else.

Michael's observation that appearances matter in academic writing is sophisticated, and sensible. However, the appearance of objectivity in academic discourse is usually not a reflection of the writer's lack of commitment to her subject and/or her propositions. This is not at all apparent to student researchers like Michael, who interpret objectivity and other conventions as merely stylistic ploys, efforts to "make everything look kosher." For Michael, this deception is reasonable because to reason effectively seems the point of the exercise, a view that, as Belenky et al. put it, involves "a curious disassociation between means and ends" (95). This Machiavellian view of academic discourse, in which commitment to beliefs and passion about the subject is secondary to giving a persuasive performance, should be no surprise. The majority of our students in Freshman English have never experienced personal commitment and passion towards their research topics. Instead they're kept busy color-coding note cards.

Halfway through their research projects, while Carrie was emerging from subjectivism, Michael seemed to have already emerged. When pressed, Carrie admitted that it *might* be possible for a researcher to say that one opinion is more valid than another. "No, I think you can," she told me. "But I don't think I do. I might. I don't know. I never thought about it." Michael, on the other hand, saw *opinion* and *fact* as closely related, not separate terms, which each involve some sort of agreement between people: "An opinion, I would have to say, is something that you have you feel there is a factual basis for. You feel enough people agree with your opinion that it can be an opinion . . . A fact is universally accepted opinion." Up until now Michael's experience with research papers, including the paper he wrote for his college Shakespeare course, told him that his task in expressing his opinions is largely procedural. He must construct a persuasive argument for his opinion (which is normally acquired before the inquiry begins), and, using collected facts and the proper stylistic conventions, he must make it sound convincing.

What Michael's experience with writing term papers seemed to have reinforced is his faith in "pure reason" (Belenky et al. 109), in which any trace of subjectivity appears to be erased. He did not even have to believe in what he was arguing, just as long as it was argued "right." It became easy, then, to choose the "correct" opinion: the one with which most people already agree. This is an approach to knowing that seems to foreclose doubt, much less dissent, and one that ultimately does little to create new knowledge. And it is also an epistemological perspective that is encouraged by the conventional, argumentative, thesis-driven research paper.

The focus on defining a thesis statement early in the writing process is standard in most textbook treatments of the assignment. It's also a message that seems to be getting through to students: Sixty-one percent of the freshman I surveyed agreed that "I have to know my thesis before I start." One implication of codifying opinion into a thesis statement—a convention that represents another bow to the scientific paradigm of research—is that students like Michael see the procedural task of research largely as lining up the right ducks, rather than entertaining conflicting claims or interpretations. Authorities' "opinions" that conflict with one's thesis are either ignored or suppressed, or simply acknowledged and then dismissed.[9] As Michael put it,

> I think it follows . . . that if you start out with your own opinion about what you're going to write about, even though you might not be consciously saying, "This is what I'm looking for" as you read your sources, you're going to sit there and say, "That has nothing to do with my topic," when you might more accurately say, "That has nothing to do with my point," [or] the opinion I have on my topic, or that [it] runs counter to my topic. I think a lot of times the tendency is to throw [counterclaims] out. . . . I think it makes it easier to think that you're writing your paper right if your opinion is correct.

Up until now, Michael managed to avoid what he terms the "hairy" task of negotiating conflicting claims by finding refuge in following the "rules" of the research paper: Come up with a thesis and then hunt for examples that support it. This hunting-and-gathering research strategy is our students' default program when faced with almost any writing assignment that involves using sources. But it's hardly what we have in mind. A study that compared how two students—one a graduate student and the other a freshman—handled their own authority in a source-based writing assignment noted that the graduate student saw examples gleaned from reading as "generative," while the freshman simply used them as "isolated" support for her opinions.

> We found it encouraging that Janet thought to use examples to help her understand her source material, but because she didn't have the goal of responding to these authors she failed to take advantage of this generative practice. . . . Examples helped her move down the ladder of abstraction, but never up, whereas they enabled Roger to run up and down the ladder at will, constructing categories at one moment, testing and illustrating key features the next. (Penrose and Geisler 514)

A pedagogy that turns texts into mines from which examples can be extracted, and students into miners who laboriously pick away at rock to find something usable, obviously does not encourage them to see knowledge as constructed. Nor does it create a particularly enticing role for themselves as knowers.

For five weeks, Carrie and Michael engaged in research projects that departed from the usual approaches to freshman research, a pedagogy that is described more fully in the next chapter. Both students were encouraged to choose their own topics, situate themselves in the center of their texts through use of the first person or, when appropriate, autobiographical digression, and consider their essays exploratory rather than necessarily argumentative. By the end of his project, Michael's perspectives on how knowledge is made and his sense of himself as a knower seemed to change significantly; but what about Carrie's perspectives?

For women, according to Belenky and her coauthors, the "quest for self and voice plays a central role in transformations in women's ways of knowing." They write that,

> [i]n a sense, each perspective we have described can be thought of as providing a new, unique training ground in which problems of self and other, inner and outer authority, voice and silence can be worked through. (133)

Like Michael, Carrie seemed to reexamine the "problems of self and other" as she struggled to position her own voice, not with, but *against*, authority. While she clung white-knuckled to her "right" to have her own opinion, and reacted to others, including authorities, who presumed to tell her she was wrong, Carrie was still grappling with her ability to *question* authority. In talking about doing so, she became momentarily self-reflective.

> It's sometimes hard to believe everything you read, whether it's a fact or not. I read a lot of articles on stuff, and I'm, like, that's not right! *I'm only a freshman in college.* . . . When I've written science papers, I've never really gone out to question anything.

If Jennifer's enlightenment about academic research was, as she told me, the importance of "questioning facts, not just summarizing them," then it seems that Carrie had at least come to share that view. By the end of her research essay project, Carrie might not yet have had the confidence to "question anything," particularly in her science writing, but she did seem to recognize that facts are open to challenge.

Research and Identity

It is now almost commonplace to hear that we are all somehow "situated" in a discourse, but since the freshman research paper first made its appearance ninety years ago, students have been instructed to mimic scientific discourse by removing any textual evidence of their "situatedness." While this isn't always an explicit instruction, the injunction against use of the first person is easily interpreted by our students to mean that research papers shouldn't be authored by people (they author themselves?). Even among the contemporary textbooks I examined, only one of the sample research papers featured in the books used first person, and then only briefly. The use of personal anecdote or observation was equally rare in sample research papers. While I don't want to suggest that the "I" and the use of explicitly autobiographical material are the only means to register authorial presence (see Chapter Four), for our students they are the most readily apparent way.

The result of a pedagogy that perpetuates the myth of objectivity, or, as Carrie put it, that forces the writer to "stand back" and transmit facts, is that it permits students to ignore the problem of situatedness. More specifically, it turns what could be a profound exercise in identity formation into an empty performance of procedural knowledge.

Drawing on the work of social psychologists, feminist theorists, anthropologists, and educators, Robert Brooke offers a theory of "identity negotiation" that might be useful here. In *Writing and Sense of Self*, Brooke maintains that identity formation arises from the tension between our internal understanding of self and our social understanding of who we're expected to be (12). In every social context, he argues, we are assigned roles that we either comply with or resist. "The pattern of individuals' stances towards the roles they are assigned (or can be assigned)," writes Brooke, "is the stuff of which identity is made" (22). These stances are negotiated; we are constantly trying to resolve competing demands about who we might be and our sense of who we are. Some of these expectations, however, we can easily escape or reject—we can choose not to join a fraternity, for example—others we want to embrace, and still others we are forced to comply with. Learning, he believes, depends on students actively negotiating their identities as they try to resolve the tensions that arise from competing social expectations about who they should be.

Brooke's theory of identity negotiation suggests that "one important focal point" in examining the composition course is "what the class establishes as writers' roles and what versions of these roles participants develop as the class progresses" (19). The writer of research papers is a role we've assigned students for years, and it is one with which they feel forced to comply, at least momentarily; but because it is not a role that engages their sense of self, there is really no need for negotiation. The assignment becomes easy to reject—"I just don't like doing research"—or misconstrue—"Researchers are formal people and I'm not a formal person." Disengaged and disinterested, feeling no dissonance at all because they're just pretending to be someone they know they're not, student writers of the traditional research paper gladly forgo the "revolution in identity" that Perry suggests accompanies epistemological growth. The "quest for self and voice" that Belenky et al. claim is central to the development of women's ways of knowing is reserved for some other, perhaps more "personal" writing assignment. And an assignment that could be central to our students developing self-conception as knowers becomes an opportunity missed.

Notes

1. A study in the early sixties of the content of eleven high school English texts reported that all but one included instruction in a "formal research project" during the senior year. The one exception featured the assignment in the junior year. Half of the texts studied, all from major publishers, included some kind of research instruction *all four years* (Lynch and Evans 302).

2. A survey was distributed to nine randomly selected sections of Freshman English at the University of New Hampshire, and administered *before* the instructors were very far into teaching the research paper (1 to 2 weeks). Students were instructed to respond to the survey based on their experience outside of their Freshman English class. The results, therefore, presumably reflect attitudes

largely shaped by the students' high school experience, and to a lesser extent, other college classes during the freshman year that required a term paper.

3. Wilson's solution to the dilemma he poses is one I endorse—the ethnographic research essay—though I believe the dilemma itself is a false one.

4. Of the eighty-four interviews with students that spanned their four years at the two schools, only two were women. Perhaps anticipating some criticism for this, Perry notes that the judges who evaluated and coded these interviews "engaged in a lively discussion of the differences between men and women" and their intellectual development. The judge concluded, however, that there was "no significant difference in locating men's and women's reports on the Chart of Development" (16).

5. Though Carrie said here that she has no problem arguing *against* an authority's claim, she admitted later that she has never done so, and might be uncomfortable trying.

6. Most students make a key distinction between knowledge in the humanities and social sciences and knowledge in the natural and physical sciences. A "fact" in political science is much less definite than a "fact" in biology, partly because the latter is viewed as more quantitative. Jehng, Johnson, and Anderson's study confirms that a student's field of study influences her epistemological beliefs. Business and engineering students, for example, view knowledge as more certain than do those in the arts or social sciences (34). A key moment in the epistemological development of our students is when they are less apt to make the distinction between "facts" in the sciences and humanities, something that occurred with both of the students I interviewed.

7. Personal experience also becomes for many students—both male and female—a means for evaluating the claims of their sources. Forty-six percent of the students I surveyed agreed or strongly agreed with this statement: "I judge an author's claims against my own experiences and observations." Only 19 percent disagreed or strongly disagreed.

8. Veysey offers a concise summary of this attitude: "The American academic scientist of the late nineteenth century usually prided himself more on the discovery of truth than on its pursuit. His goal was certainty—not a labyrinth of tentative opinions or opinions true only for the people of one time or place. He was unable to partake of a thoroughgoing relativism, although if his studies concerned human behavior he was capable of making intermittent nods in what would later be termed a relativist direction" (145). The scientific paradigm adopted by most academic researchers led to a kind of dogmatism about one's discoveries that, according to Veysey, accounted for disagreements as ignorance of the "facts" (146–7).

9. Almost half of the students surveyed (44 percent) in the writing program I surveyed agreed or strongly agreed with the statement "I look primarily for information that supports my point of view" when they approach sources for their research papers. Slightly more than a quarter of the students (27 percent) disagreed or strongly disagreed with that statement.

Three

"An Amateur's Raid in a World of Specialists"
The Essayist as Researcher

So it is no good our mounting on stilts, for even on stilts we have to walk with our own legs; and upon the most exalted throne in the world it is still our own bottom that we sit on.
—Michel de Montaigne, *Essays*

In early April, Michael and Carrie's composition instructors explained the details of the research assignment. Class members would divide into smaller groups, and each group would agree on a general topic of study relating to television, a theme of the course. Then every student would choose a "subtopic" of their group's subject for an individual research project and paper. Later, each group would make a collaborative presentation, and each member would report on his or her individual research.

The paper was not to be a research *report*, the instructors emphasized, but rather an *essay* that incorporated their own ideas about the topic. They were expected to take some sort of "position" on it. The essay did not need to be formally structured, and they were invited to use the first person. "I want them to get into the mud of research," Erika, one of the instructors told me, "and get them excited about being part of the cog and wheels of university life. . . . I don't give two hoots about how formal it is." She added,

> I want them to understand how their voice fits into the voices of other researcher/thinkers dealing with similar ideas. It's all about seeing how they fit themselves into other things—what they stand in relation to. I guess it's the same sort of idea as the essays we make them write—it's about wanting them to think about them- selves, take themselves seriously. And the research paper (ideally) makes them think about themselves vis-a-vis other people/thinkers in an academic community. But perhaps I'm too idealistic.

What is striking about Erika's pedagogy is not its idealism, but its dramatic departure from conventional approaches to the research pa- per. The image of research here is relational—"I want them to see how their voice fits into the voices of other researcher/thinkers"—and "richly peopled" (Frey 33), rather than adversarial and impersonal. It is also unapologetically subjective. What Erika hopes is that her stu- dents will "think about themselves" in relation to others through their research; the self is to be seen as an active agent, dialogically involved in listening and responding "to other voices," and in the process trans- forming and being transformed, "seeing how they fit themselves into other things." To do this, however, students must "take themselves seriously." They must believe in their own voices.

For Carrie, and perhaps for most committed subjectivists, at first this doesn't seem like any problem at all. She can't imagine writing a formal research paper in which she isn't allowed to express herself: "I think that if I had to write a paper and I couldn't put my opinion in at all, I would have a lot of trouble." Michael, on the other hand, is not so sure. An experienced hand at writing "dry" and "impersonal" re- search papers, he confesses that "this research paper is taking me a lit- tle off the beaten path." He adds, "I'm starting to develop my own voice very recently, so it's kind of weird now taking a research paper and doing it that way. It will be an experience writing this paper, I'm sure."

Their instructors' invitation to see the research paper as an exten- sion of the personal essay writing Michael and Carrie have been doing all semester long will ultimately create separate challenges for each student, something I explore later in this chapter and in the next. Car- rie will come to recognize that, at times, her attentiveness to her own voice makes it difficult for her to hear others' voices. Michael's sophis- ticated understanding of the rhetoric of conventional research papers, which once protected him from any strong commitment to his beliefs, will be subverted by his adoption of what he comes to call an "essay- istic" stance. Among other things, as we've already seen, Michael will find the need to take responsibility for his ideas bewildering, scary. But both students will come to see their conceptions of themselves as writers, a role they claimed earlier in the course, will be enlarged and challenged as they try to adapt it to the task of writing with sources.

Drawing on Michael and Carrie's experiences, along with those of other students, I argue in this chapter for a different approach to introducing students to college research. Like the pedagogy Erika espoused, it is an approach that builds on the writing that came before it, is relational rather than adversarial, and is exploratory rather than exclusively explanatory and argumentative. It also openly acknowledges the writer–researcher's subjectivity in a way that is more likely to encourage student writers like Michael and Carrie to experience the "revolution in identity" that Perry believes is a mark of intellectual growth. While this introduction to research writing may include some of the features of the historical assignment, including a concern for teaching certain conventions, such as citation, its aims are less to teach students to model academic discourse than to introduce them to some of the habits of mind that are fundamental to academic inquiry. I will contend that these habits of mind are often already practiced by students in many writing process courses from the first day; we simply failed to recognize it, and missed the chance to make the research paper assignment an integral part of what they *already* do.

What Bridges the Abyss?

Lying in a hammock one day last summer, I reread *The Making of Meaning* from cover to cover—the first time I'd read Ann Berthoff in some years—and I could see the many ways her work shaped my thinking and teaching. It was a timely encounter. I had just read Matthew Wilson's provocative article "Research, Expressivism, and Silence" in which he wonders why some students seem to struggle "to switch gears" from personal writing to academic writing. "It is here, at this juncture, between an expressivist composition pedagogy and the research paper," writes Wilson, "that the silence falls" (251). While Wilson finds that the two pedagogies create an "impossible transition," Berthoff reminds us of what they may have in common.

> The abyss that opens up between the fall semester and the spring semester, between English 101 and English 102, between personal writing and expository writing, between "free writing" and "guided structured writing"—all these gaps result inevitably when we try to teach according to some linear model in which something allegedly simple must come before something allegedly complex. Pedagogy always echoes epistemology: the way we teach reflects the conception we have of what knowledge is and does, the way we think

about thinking. Using the categories of the Old Rhetoric as models for theme assignments keeps us from showing our students *the essential acts of mind that are necessarily involved, no matter what kind of writing is being done.* (11; emphasis added)

The key to bridging the abyss, Berthoff advises, is that "elements of what we want to end with must be present in some form from the start." The fissure between personal writing and research writing, into which students like Jayne may fall, might not be the inevitable gap between "incompatible pedagogies," as Wilson argues, but rather our failure to clarify to our students what it is we are asking them to do in the research paper that they have been doing all along. Granted, the research assignment creates some challenges that the personal narrative does not, but Berthoff urges us to find what are the "essential acts of mind" present in *both* kinds of writing and thinking. What habits of mind are introduced the first day of English 101 that might also present the last day of English 102?

While trying to name these intellectual practices, I kept returning to five perspectives that seemed to bridge the abyss, things that are present "in some form" in the very first assignments I give in E 101 as well as the last assignments in E 102, the research writing course at my university. They are

1. The willingness to suspend judgment
2. The ability to tolerate ambiguity
3. The understanding that inquiry is driven by questions, not answers
4. The recognition that writing is a mode of thought, that writing can make meaning rather than simply report it
5. The belief that meaning-making is a dialectical process

As I look over this list, I easily imagine the ways in which I attempt to enact these practices when I encourage students to write personal essays at the beginning of E 101. When I ask them to freewrite about a personal experience, I am asking them to suspend judgment and indulge in the pleasures of writing as a mode of thought. As they write about their lives, I encourage them to choose experiences to explore *not* because they already understand how they feel or what they think about them but because they want to find out. I encourage them to embrace confusion and see questions as the way to direct their personal explorations and writing as a means to discover what they didn't know they knew. As they compose personal narratives, I ask them to deploy the dialectics of *what happened* and *what happens,* their *observations of* things and their *ideas about* them, between *showing* and *telling,* *specifics* and *generalities,* between the *sea of their experience* and the *mountain of reflection* from which they can see the pattern in the waves. It was the movement back and forth between these ways of seeing and thinking that produced Jayne's insightful essay "The Sterile Cage"; it is a dialectic that is most likely to produce personal essays that transcend the particulars of a writer's individual experience and allow him to begin to account for it as a category of experience. It is how we make meaning.

Isn't this exactly the process that is at the heart of academic inquiry? Don't we often begin with questions and see more questions as the welcome fallout of continuing the investigation, further complicating what we thought we knew? And doesn't this require that we suspend judgment, finding in the ambiguity about what might be true a kind of thrill that drives us forward? Isn't most research a fundamentally dialectical process—collecting evidence and developing ideas about what it means, then collecting more evidence and refining these ideas? And for many of us, the act of writing is an integral part of this making sense of things.

Unfortunately, all of this is rarely evident from our published scholarship—particularly to our students—because it so often masks the process that went into the reporting of our conclusions. The historic paradigm that governs the teaching of the freshman research paper also does not lead students to understand the open-ended nature of inquiry. In fact, the research paper frequently stands in the way of this understanding, reducing the research process into a picking of sides and a selective hunt for evidence, or an "objective" report in the paste-pot and shears tradition. The researcher need not suspend judgment, because she's already made up her mind. There is no need to experience ambiguity, because it disrupts the orderly march towards a conclusion. Writing is relegated to small note cards. And the dialectic of discovery moves in a single direction—from generalities to specifics, down the ladder of abstraction but rarely up, and certainly not moving much in either direction.

This all helps me understand that Jayne's failure to negotiate the move from her touching and insightful personal essays to her wooden and uninspired research paper was not the incompatibility of expressive and academic writing, but my failure to fashion a research assignment that helped her use and extend what she had already done so well—for it was in the beginning of the course, when Jayne first began to essay her experiences, that she was learning the true spirit of inquiry.

How Montaigne Refused to Write Research Reports

I like to imagine that Michel de Montaigne, who first coined the word *essai* to describe his experiments in self-reflective writing, was among the first writers to bristle like our students at the fifteenth-century version of the traditional research paper. As a Renaissance schoolboy, Montaigne received a classical education. He was fluent in Latin and familiar with the models of classical rhetoric. He was schooled in the extensive use of quotes and adages from ancient Authority as an unquestioned source of wisdom and truth. In short, Montaigne was educated to write the conventional Renaissance research paper—formal in language and structure, well planned, and composed with ancient sources whose authority was well established and whose words reflected accepted truths. As an adult writer of essays, however, Montaigne actively rebelled against the scholastic tradition of his schooling. J. M. Cohen, who edited a popular translation of Montaigne's essays, observed that Montaigne "seldom read books through, but preferred to dip into them in search of arguments, anecdotes, and observations that threw light on his current interests."

> He did not care for the apparatus of learning, with its lengthy
> preliminaries, its strictly marshalled pleadings and proofs. He was
> always impatient to come quickly to the heart of the matter. (15)

If anything, Montaigne's essays represent an utter disregard for the dominant conventions, or as noted Montaigne critic Hugo Friedrich put it, "the most extreme antitype to Latin humanist prose" in its "determined abandonment of composition," particularly the formal arrangements of classical rhetoric (336). Montaigne's "antischolastic tendencies" (353) were partly playful irreverence, but more importantly they reflected epistemological challenges issued by a man who was no longer content with the truth of received knowledge. In other words, Montaigne got tired of writing research reports and wanted to write research essays.

The open form that Montaigne devised grows very much from the word he chose to describe it: the *essai* is an experiment, an attempt, and the *essaier*, one who take risks. The essayist, no longer certain of received truth, is no longer able to pretend certainty: "Could my mind find a firm footing I should not be making essays, but coming to conclusions" (235). The essay itself, then, becomes exploratory rather than explanatory, tentative rather than conclusive, much more concerned with the process of thought than with the product, and enacted more as a conversation with readers than as a treatise. In these ways, it departed not only from the classical rhetorical tradition, but also from the scientific positivism which the learned embraced centuries later.

Above all, its epistemological assumptions distinguished Montaigne's essay from the more conventional rhetorical forms. Authority, he believed, should always be approached skeptically—"I hold that truth is no wiser for being old" (364)—and while Montaigne never ceased citing sayings of the ancients in his essays, he was careful to point out they are meant to serve his own thinking: "I only quote others to make myself more explicit" (52). In keeping with this skepticism about the truth of received knowledge, Montaigne was also a social constructionist. "Our opinions are grafted one on another," he observes. "The first serves as stock for the second, the second for the third. We thus climb the ladder, step by step" (349). However, his vision of the making of knowledge is one that may allow for learning from the learned, but most of all celebrates direct experience as the best teacher.[1] Rather than chasing after "bookish examples," Montaigne advises that in the "most familiar and commonplace events" one can discover "the most marvelous examples" that can "make our testimony convincing" if we "could but see them in their right light" (364). He believed that the great variety and diversity of experience will reveal the world's disunity rather than its "connectedness and conformity" (358), as laws, theories, and principles seem to wrongly suggest. Montaigne reminded us that as much as we may seek a transcendent understanding of the world by "mounting on stilts," it is our corporeal experience that makes knowledge meaningful and true for us: ". . . and upon the most exalted throne in the world it is still our own bottom that we sit on" (406).

Scholars of the Self

Ultimately Montaigne's epistemology—like Huck's—is one that honors lived experience as a way to evaluate the truth of received knowledge. But he also views experience as a valuable *source* of knowledge if only we become scholars of the self as well as the world. There is nothing certain about what we learn, though; our judgements about the personal and the worldly are always provisional. According to Montaigne, as time passes everything is in flux—"the world is a perpetual seesaw"—including the self, which is "always restless" (235). He writes,

> I cannot fix my subject. . . . I do not portray his being; I portray his passage; not a passage from one age to another . . . but from day to day, minute to minute. I must suit my story to the hour, for soon I may change, not only by chance but also by intention. It is a record of various and variable occurrences, an account of thoughts that are unsettled and, as chance will have it, at times contradictory, either because I am then another self, or because I approach my subject under different circumstances and with other considerations. (235)

For Montaigne, subjectivity is fluid, in part a product of intention, in part inscribed by circumstance and situation, but always changing. He further elaborates on the shifting nature of the self by suggesting that it is also constructed by language; he writes of his collection of essays, for example, that "I have no more made my book than my book has made me" (quoted in Friedrich 329).

For the essayist, then, to come to know means the knower cannot separate herself from the situation that gives rise to the need to know. Who is she at that moment? How might that influence her perceptions? Why does she want to know? What does her own experience tell her might be true? And especially, *how* does she come to know, and what are her reflections on those revelations? Hugo Friedrich writes that it

> is one of the fundamental features of the essay that it does not separate the subject about which it is speaking from the personal conditions that led the author to that subject, nor does it separate it from the associate links it has to other subjects. The *occasions of reflection*, regardless of how and why they originate, are also preserved in that reflection. (346; emphasis added)

It is the writer's awareness of his *situatedness*, to use a poststructuralist term, that seems crucial to the Montaignian essay, and this awareness is often explicitly revealed to the reader. In fact, Montaigne has little faith in the authority of any writers or speakers who do not reveal a high level of self-awareness, who conceal themselves "behind a mask, without the courage to show oneself as one is" (208). In "On Presumption," Montaigne observes that in a relativistic world, he cannot fully believe the truth of a claim unless its proponent perceives that self-knowledge is as worthy a pursuit as worldly knowledge. Put differently, Montaigne believes that self-reflexivity both enables us as knowers and makes what we know more believable to others. If I cannot claim to know myself, Montaigne asks, how can I persuasively claim to know the world?

> I find an extreme variety of opinions, an intricate labyrinth of difficulties, one on top of another, and a very great uncertainty and diversity in the school of wisdom itself. Seeing therefore that these people have been unable to agree on their knowledge of themselves and of their condition, which is constantly before their eyes, and is within themselves; seeing that they do not know how these things move that they themselves set in motion, nor how to describe and explain to us the springs that they themselves hold and manage, you may judge how little I can believe them when they set out the causes of the rise and fall of the Nile. (193)

In the universe of the essay, there is a "deeper" knowing than reason, argument, and the methods of proof. There is, as Kurt Spellmeyer put it, a knowledge that gives essayists more than "one gospel or another"; rather, it assists them "in their particular struggles to decide who they have been and what they will become" ("Language" 281).

It is also, I would add, a genre which, when deployed in the place of the conventional research paper, makes this a personal struggle over epistemological beliefs. As students measure their own voices against those in sources, they confront their relationship to authority—"In what ways do my opinions matter?"—and to truth—"How do I know what to believe?" The self-reflexive nature of the essay makes these questions almost inescapable.

The Essay as a Mode of Inquiry

The essay genre as Montaigne conceived it seems a useful alternative to the traditional freshman research paper on many grounds, especially epistemological ones. The essay offers an opposing theory of knowledge from the scientific paradigm valorized by the research ideal, and it also seems more consistent with much current thinking about the nature of knowledge. While the essay does not fully embrace the epistemic view of knowledge articulated by most poststructuralists, because it lends more weight to authorial intention and agency, the Montaignian view is that knowledge is a social construction and truth never certain. The essayist never pretends to be objective in the never-ending search for truth, but recognizes—as most postmodern theorists do—that our perceptions are shaped by our circumstances and "conditions," and that the self, like the knowledge one seeks, is unstable and difficult to fix. Because of the instability of knowledge and subjectivity, the essayist recognizes that whatever truth he discerns is momentary.

While the essay genre may be an alternative to the positivism that seems to be the epistemological core of conventional approaches to the research paper, it also seems to oppose much disciplinary writing in its resistance to systematic thought—"It proceeds, so to speak, methodically unmethodically" (Adorno 161). In "The Essay as Form," T. W. Adorno observes that the essay defies the "unanimity of logical order," which in conventional arguments or treatises can deceive readers into believing that ideas are neatly hierarchical or reality whole. He writes that "[the essay] thinks in fragments just as reality is fragmented and gains its unity only by moving through the fissures rather than smoothing them over" (164). The essayist "gropes" at the pieces of what might be known rather than pretending to grasp the whole.

> Thus the essay distinguishes itself from a scientific treatise. He writes essayistically who writes while experimenting, who turns his object this way and that, who questions it, feels it, tests it, thoroughly reflects on it, attacks it from different angles, and in his mind's eye collects what he sees, and puts into words what the

object allows to be seen under the conditions established in the
course of the writing. (Bense, quoted in Adorno 164)

What Adorno celebrates here is an approach to inquiry that is
never stripped of the context that gives it meaning, and has an almost
playful quality that allows the suspension of judgment and the pro-
longing of doubt, which are among the perspectives I proposed earlier
as central to inquiry. In the essay, there is less need to *prove* an assertion than to explore its possible meanings, and this is a departure from
what William Zeiger calls the "scientific model of thesis and support"
that dominates the teaching of the essay—and I'd argue especially the
research paper—in most composition classrooms. Though the essay
has long been the primary genre of Freshman English, Zeiger argues
that the essays of Montaigne are "distinct in kind from those we demand of our composition students today."

> To "prove" an assertion today is to win undisputed acceptance for
> it—to stop inquiry rather than start it. There is nothing tentative or
> playful in this action; we "prove" an idea not to learn about it, but
> to fix it in certainty. . . . When one sets out to prove an assertion
> in the modern sense, one tolerates no ambiguity; every hint of
> variance from the preferred line of thought must be solidly re-
> jected. (456–7)

I am not suggesting here that the methods of argument shouldn't
be taught in Freshman English, or that argument should never be a
feature of academic research. But what students rarely perceive about
academic writing is that a structured argument is the *product* of inquiry, and that the *process* of inquiry that preceded it often invites complexity, ambiguity, and playfulness. Academic inquiry frequently
demands that we suspend judgment about what might be true, and
embrace a dialectical process that might lead us to new understandings. Using published scholarship as a model for the freshman research
paper, or teaching the formal research paper as we've inherited it, is, I
believe, unlikely to teach students these habits of mind. In fact, those
approaches may encourage students to get the wrong idea about researching. Instead, it is the extension of *essaying*—a mode of thought
many of us introduce in the first days of E 101—that can be the best
introduction to academic inquiry. It offers freshmen the invitation to
experience that playfulness and uncertainty that both motivates researchers and gives them pleasure. The exploratory research *essay*,
rather than the argumentative research paper, makes the introduction
to inquiry—and the process of coming to know—central aims of the
assignment rather than focusing exclusively a written product that follows academic conventions.

The Rhetoric of the Research Essay

Admittedly, the essayistic approach to research I'm proposing does not model traditional academic writing particularly well. It is, if anything, almost "extra-disciplinary," argues R. Lane Kaufmann, in its determination "not to stay within the well-charted boundaries of academic disciplines, not to shuttle back and forth across these boundaries, but to reflect on them and challenge them" (90). Graham Good adds that "the essay celebrates diversity when the disciplines seek unity." The essay, he says, "presents 'special' instances to the 'general' reader, where disciplines present 'general' conclusions to the 'specialist'" (6). Scott Russell Sanders, a personal essayist often anthologized in composition readers, observes that the essay represents "an amateur's raid in a world of specialists" ("Singular First Person" 190). Sanders' characterization of the essay literally describes the experience of college freshmen who undertake academic research, but it also suggests a wholly different rhetorical situation for students than the one created by the conventional research paper, one that I think is more useful.

In his account of the history of the APA *Publication Manual*, Charles Bazerman notes that its steady growth in pages and detailed prescriptions for manuscript preparation coincided with the rise of behaviorist psychology, which sought not to describe the mind, but to quantify behavior. This led to what Bazerman called "incremental encyclopedism," or an approach to gathering knowledge, the aim of which was to simply add narrow descriptive facts—"to fill gaps in other results"—rather than "trying to find answers to theoretical questions" (139). The "rhetorical consequences" of this approach are some of the familiar features of the formal research papers taught to students: introductions that are summaries of existing factual knowledge rather than a discussion of a problem, a thesis pushed to the front of the article, formal and often specialized language, and (at least in the case of the APA) the author–date citation, which reinforces the "incrementalism of the literature" (139–40).

Bazerman writes,

> Only when a community decides that there is one right way can it achieve the confidence and narrowness of detailed prescriptions. In rhetoric, "one right way" implies not only a stability of text, but a stability of rhetorical situation and rhetorical actors, so that there is little room or motive for improvisatory argument. Within a stabilized rhetorical universe, people will want to say similar things to each other under similar conditions for similar purposes. In this context, prescribed forms allow easy and efficient communication without unduly constraining needed flexibility. The behaviorist picture of the world allows that stability and lack of free invention. (137)

The open form of the research essay seems the antithesis to the "lack of free invention" and "improvisatory argument" that characterizes the rhetoric of conventional academic research Bazerman describes. While the writer of formal research assumes a "stabilized rhetorical universe," the writer of the research essay assumes a range of "rhetorical actors" whom one may not assume have "similar things to say." While the purpose of the formal academic paper is to "fill gaps" in existing knowledge, the purpose of the research essay is to experiment with new ways of seeing existing knowledge, to find out rather than to prove. "Incremental encyclopedism" asks readers to consider primarily the results, while essaying draws readers' attention to the person who tentatively suggests them. In the formal research paper, one gains acceptance by following the rules of presentation (Bazerman, "Codifying" 139). In the essay, the writer discovers an appropriate form through conversation—with herself, with her subject, and with her readers. In the traditional research paper, reason rules; in the essay, the writer's intuition and personality is predominant (Zeiger 461).

The problem with the rhetorical discourse of the formal research paper (and many of its less formal variations) is that it is in response to an exigency that students do not yet recognize as real: the need to fill gaps in existing knowledge, to prove results to an audience of fellow experts, to gain acceptance by a particular discourse community. Perhaps they should. Certainly David Bartholomae thinks so when he argues that students must "try on the peculiar ways of knowing, selecting, evaluating, reporting, concluding, and arguing that define the discourse of our community" ("Inventing" 134). However, many students feel forced to conform to this role, and as a result, they disengage themselves from it. "What you write begins to distance itself from you—become unfamiliar with your true feelings," said one student as she reflected on Bartholomae's call to model academic discourse. "[T]he student capable of conforming to the ideologies of the university will succeed. Those that stay firm on their own feelings, unable to conform, will no doubt fail. How sad!"

What *does* seem real to first-year students is a rhetorical discourse that is created in response to a more urgent, and often personal, need to find out about something, to ask meaningful questions that research can help answer. By making the appropriation of knowledge personal, the essay introduces students to the real drama of inquiry: negotiating the tension between what their own experience and intuition tells them is true and what someone else tells them is true. And when we ask students to explore this tension by writing about it in their own words, without pretending to be objective or certain or even original, they may begin to see that knowledge making is not about following rules but making conversation.

The emphasis on teaching procedural knowledge—the formal structure of academic research, the methods of proof, the stylistic conventions—reflected in traditional research paper instruction, and lately in pedagogies proposed by proponents of teaching academic discourse, removes the tension that inspires genuine inquiry. When writing teachers insist that students strip away any visible evidence of their "situatedness," by asking that they pretend or forget or leave behind the experiences and discourses that defined who they are and how they speak so that they can learn "ours," makes it easy for them to lower the stakes of the encounter. Writing term papers then becomes the familiar game of "pleasing the teacher." As one student put it, "We are the ones who always need to reach for the professor. . . . We as students know we need to control the language, but what we have to find out is how to do it in order to please the teacher."

On the other hand, the research *essay* insists that the students' encounter with other voices and other views is constantly filtered through their own "perspectives and presuppositions, and not with their disciplined suppression" (Spellmeyer, *Common Ground* 110). As Spellmeyer observes,

> [T]eachers should recognize that English 101, with its tolerance for essayistic introspection and digression, is probably the only opportunity most students will ever have to discover the relationship of mutual implication, a relationship fundamental to all writing, between the self and the cultural heritage within which selfhood has meaning. To put it in the simplest terms, we do not deny the socially constituted nature of learning or identity when we ask our students to write from their own situations, but I believe it is both dishonest and disabling to pretend that writing, no matter how formal or abstract, is not created by persons, from within the contexts—historical, social, intellectual, institutional—of their lived experience. (110)

In "Singular First Person," his essay on essay writing, Scott Sanders writes that readers are drawn to the genre because they "feel overwhelmed by data, random information, the flotsam and jetsam of mass culture" and they "relish the spectacle of a single consciousness making sense of a portion of the chaos" (190). When we ask students to use themselves—their own situations, their own "consciousness"—as the organizing principle of their research projects in Freshman English, they are more likely to ask the question that pragmatist William James insisted is at the heart of inquiry: "Grant an idea or belief to be true . . . what concrete difference will its being true make in anyone's actual life?" (97). And by asking this question, students produce writing that readers will want to read. But it also creates writing that is not the specialized discourse of the disciplines, with its concern for results that fill gaps and construction of convincing proofs, but a more public discourse that attempts to locate the meaning of disciplinary knowledge in people's lives. The research essay revives a rhetoric of public discourse that S. Michael Halloran believes should find its way back into composition instruction, and that Spellmeyer argues will promote an "ethic of mutual understanding" (*Common Ground* 22) that has been made more difficult by the fragmentation of knowledge into disciplines.

Isn't it far better that we initiate our students into academic research through a genre that reminds them of the meaningfulness of knowledge rather than its remoteness, and encourages them to look across disciplines for it? By urging them to write in a way that narrows the gap between their own language and the language of experts, don't we make it more likely that the words they choose will allow them to appropriate, not be appropriated by, specialized discourses? And by urging them to produce research writing that people will want to read, don't we remind them of the importance of doing research that matters?

Solving the "Problem" of Subjectivity

I liked the eighth grade and was loathe to leave it. I took typing in summer school with my old friends, a kind of last hurrah before moving on to the big public high school several blocks away. When high school began, it felt like nothing I had done before had much to do with what I was being asked to do. I was lost, invisible among six hundred other high school freshmen. I tried out for the swim team because my brother was a star in the hundred-yard butterfly. I was cut the first day of tryouts. When I spoke in class, I almost didn't recognize my own voice—it was thin, pathetically hopeful. I got C's mostly. English was my worse subject. I think of high school like a lot of people do—as a time when adolescents try on identities like clothes from the rack, most of which are ill-fitting and awkward. I spent those years shopping around for a good fit like everyone else, and trying desperately to make my presence felt—in class, on the track team, at the make-out parties. What I didn't realize was what Dorothy in *The Wizard of Oz* learned from her bump on the head: I didn't need to travel so far to find out how to get home.

I think of this now as I try to describe what happens to my students when they first try to essay their research. While they may have felt at home with autobiographical writing, they find the invitation to establish a similar presence in source-based writing exciting at first, and then daunting. They wonder at the weakness of their voices, at the sudden sense of anonymity. Some shout to overcompensate, seizing a soapbox and producing a monologic draft that's all opinion. Others resort to "patch writing," producing drafts that simply report factual information for five or so paragraphs, then veer to one or two paragraphs of opinion before they return to reporting. Some simply resort to what they know best about research writing—pretending to be "objective" by deliberately erasing any evidence of authorship, avoiding the problem of subjectivity altogether. They knew in their hearts they wouldn't make the swim team anyway.

Carrie's draft research essay on whether *The Simpson's* has any social value is, in many ways, representative of the kinds of problems many students have when they try to "stick in" their own views, rather than exploit the opportunity the essay offers to "work out" what they think is a more dialogic relationship with their sources. Like many students, Carrie coded her entry into the text by signaling that she is about to comment by using stock phrases—"In my opinion" and "I'd have to say, to me, . . ." These phrases typically appear in student papers preceding some broad statements of belief, statements often only loosely tethered to information the researcher has gathered. The location of opinions is also telling. Usually, they are placed at the end of a paragraph of mostly factual information, in isolated paragraphs in the body of the paper, or at the very end. There is no elaboration of the ideas, no qualification, no substantiation, no exploration. Opinions serve more as a broad summary of beliefs, especially the student's simple agreement or disagreement with an authority's claims. The writer has a presence, but it is not as one who is dialectically engaged with the information she has gathered. She is more a hesitant bystander, forced to speak out in class.

I get the sense reading passages like these that students view this kind of insertion of opinion as an obligatory move. Though they are at first taken with the openly subjective nature of the research essay, they find in practice that it is awkward and difficult to say what they think, particularly when their voices are posed against those of experts. They are struggling for their own authority as knowers, or, to borrow from Bahktin, they are struggling *against* the colonizing power of "authoritative discourse." While my editorial antennae twitch when seeing phrases like "in my opinion"—and they should probably be cut in the next draft—behind those unnecessary words is perhaps a necessary epistemological move: It often is the sound of a writer who is measuring the timber of her own voice. As Mina Shaugnessy alerted us to the logic of the grammatical errors of basic writers, we must also be alert to logic of the awkward writing in student research papers, particularly how it reveals issues of authority.

But Carrie presents a complicated case. Is she struggling to establish her own authority in her paper, or is she simply announcing it?

Since Carrie is a relativist committed to the belief that "every one is entitled to their own opinion," and she is at times resistant to the "right" of authorities to claim that their judgements are more true, the research essay would seem to suit her perfectly. It offers the soapbox I mentioned earlier.

However, did Carrie enact the essay genre as I've described it? Unlike Michael, Carrie noted that she does not see the research process as an opportunity to explore a topic. "I usually decide what I think [before I start]," she told me. Carrie's enactment of the research essay form, then, does not exploit one of its most prominent features—the desire to *find out* rather than to prove. Lacking the willingness to withhold judgment, and especially to see uncertainty as the condition of inquiry, students like Carrie often revert back to the hunting-and-gathering approach to research: look for "opinions" in sources that "back up" what you already think. Carrie did tell me that she would have considered using views that conflicted with hers had she found any. But she was relieved she didn't because it made the paper "easier to write." She added, "If I had encountered [a view that conflicted with hers], I would have put it in there, but then I would have been battling with an imaginary person on the paper." Had Carrie approached her topic more like an essayist, listening more attentively to other voices because she hopes to learn what she thinks, the shift in her relationship to authority might have allowed her to see a conversation where she only saw a battle.

My point is this: Some of the difficulties students have with the problem of presence in the research essay derive, I think, from their genuine confusion about genre. When I ask them to write a research *essay* rather than a research paper, they aren't sure what I mean, so they devise a kind of mixed genre—it is subjective, even autobiographical at times, but it also argues from the thesis-example model. Lacking the structure and tone of a formal paper, however, they struggle with ways to make that argument, and especially how and where to express their "opinions."[2] (In the next chapter, I propose that one way to help them negotiate their authority in the research essay is to refocus them on the act of note taking.)

While critics of personal writing in the composition class may seize on my account of student struggles with the research essay as evidence of the dangers of solipsism, I have come to see the difficulty some students have with the problem of subjectivity as a key step to their understanding of inquiry, one that is too easy to avoid in the formal research paper. In fact, the ways students resolve the dilemma of *how* to establish a presence in the research essay turns out, I think, to be one of its most instructive features. As they attempt to bridge what they practiced in essay writing with what they are asked to do in the researched essay, students reassess their rhetorical situation, their assumptions about the nature of research, and sometimes reevaluate their epistemological beliefs. They must try on a new identity as knowers, as writers in charge of sorting through and making sense of other people's knowledge as they try to make it their own.

While students like Carrie may initially respond to the challenge of managing her authority in her research essay by producing a kind of mixed-genre paper—part conventional research paper and part personal opinion essay—they can be coached to see the value of enacting a conversation with their sources *from the very beginning* of the research process. "Opinion" then emerges more naturally from this conversation. It is not a static thing, but is instead shaped by each encounter. And as their opinions are shaped, so is their sense of themselves as knowers, actively engaged in making sense of things. What students then discover is that they can reclaim that sense of self they felt so at home with in autobiographical writing, yet expand its boundaries.

Michael Finds His North Star

Michael, with his keen sense of the rhetoric of school writing, recognizes this immediately as he begins to approach his research paper on the exploitation of women in TV advertising "essayistically" rather than using the "cold, hard system" of the formal research paper. Michael observes, for example, that when he began his first draft, he struggled to feel comfortable with "where [he] was coming from."

> I didn't know how formal a voice to use because it was still a
> "Research Paper." [My first attempt] was dry. Very, very up on my
> horse. It wasn't what I wanted to write. It's not what I've been
> writing all semester. And I don't think it will wash for this. I think
> . . . the way I'm coming at this from an essay standpoint, as
> opposed to a research paper, is making it easier.

Michael's experience with the "objective" report of the conventional research paper clashes with his sense that essay, as he has practiced it all semester, demands something else. The dissonance he feels grows from his anxiety over genre—what kind of writing should this be?—but I don't think he is resolving that dissonance by choosing to conform to expectations imposed on him, which is typical of the rhetorical decisions students make when writing term papers, particularly in matters of voice. "It wasn't what *I* wanted to write," he says. Michael implies here a commitment not only to his project, and his desire to communicate about it clearly, something that did not require getting high on his horse.[3] Freed from the need to give the *appearance* of authority and certainty that the conventional research paper implies, Michael discovers that the essay suddenly alters his relationship to his audience:

> I feel like I'm almost having *a conversation* with my reader about television and the implications of advertising. . . . [With] the old approach, I felt like a teacher, like a lecturer, standing before a whole lot of people who didn't want to be there, because I didn't really want to be there. For this, I felt a lot more involved. . . . Being able to say "I" left me so much room to put a little bit of me into the paper, as opposed to just "this was," "it is". . . I'd have to say that it makes it easier for the reader to identify with you because it seems a lot more like a conversation, because you're letting yourself think and feel, so I think it tends to let the reader think and feel.

The way Michael constructs the rhetorical situation as an essayist is profoundly different from the "cold, hard" world of the formal research paper; it is, in James Moffett's words, a much more "realistic communication 'drama'" (12) that involves a genuine "interaction among communicants." That interaction is lacking, Moffett argues, when audience is an abstraction, or is perceived as uninterested in the message, as is often the case with the traditional research paper. But when the writer imagines she is speaking to someone—something the essay genre encourages—she is more motivated, because the purpose of the communication is more compelling. "Put into the drama of somebody with something to say to somebody else" (12), she can grasp not only *what* she is writing about, but *what for:* to reach a real audience. Moffett characterizes these two contrasting rhetorical situations as the "I–you"—one that emphasizes the relationship between speaker and listener—and the "I–it"—a relationship between speaker and subject. "A whole, authentic discourse," maintains Moffett, involves the "crossing" of both (31).

> Rhetoric, or the art of acting on someone through words, is an abstractive act. That is, one performs the same activities in pitching a subject to an audience as one does in extracting that subject from raw phenomena: one selects and reorganizes traits of things, digests, codes preferentially. . . . Both abstracting *from* and abstracting *for* concern the same kinds of choice. The difference is whether the speaker–subject relation or the speaker–listener relation is determining the choice—the extracting from the source or the anticipation of audience response. (32)

By abandoning the rhetorical structure of the formal research paper, Michael is now allowing the "I–you"—or the speaker–listener relation—to begin determining the choices he makes about how to write his essay, but without abandoning the "I–it" relation, his own working out of what he makes of his topic. He is conversing, both with himself and his readers, and this dialogue is structuring his thought. There is a genuine "crossing" in the research essay between these two relations that is lacking in the traditional paper, with its emphasis on *abstracting from* rather than *abstracting for*. Unable yet to imagine the members of a particular discourse community as a real audience, freshmen find that the research essay creates a real audience of peers—not specialists—that preserves the "drama" of the writing situation. This strikes me as a much more logical and natural initiation into research than the sudden shift to the much more artificial rhetorical situation of the formal research paper or discipline-specific writing.

Michael, then, resolves the problem of presence in his research essay by restructuring the rhetorical situation. But he also begins to see inquiry differently: "This is the first time I've written a 'fact-based' paper where I didn't feel that I already knew what my answer was going to be when I started." Rather than trying to "sell a point," he finds that the essayistic approach allows him to come to the project with "a beginner's mind." Part of this, apparently, is Michael's willingness to put up with a degree of uncertainty, and even a temporary lack of focus—something he already learned earlier in the semester that is a natural part of the process of writing essays. Interestingly, he sees this essayistic stance in research writing as embracing both objectivity *and* subjectivity.

> [The unfocused stage is valuable] because I think it's going to let me be a lot more—and it's always put in quotes—"objective" as far as what I'm getting [from sources]. I won't be saying, this is good, I agree with this, this is something I need to read. And it won't be, this is bad, they didn't go about it right because they disagree with me, *because I don't know who I am yet, and I don't know where I stand on the issue.*

The essay allows Michael to withhold judgement, and as a result, he believes he reads more objectively, weighing and evaluating sources rather than judging them based on a preconceived opinion about what is true. The task is no longer about lining up ducks, but seeing where they fly. The research essay, then, encourages Michael to be both objective *and* subjective. He accounts for how his own situation determines what he thinks and feels, but by tolerating a certain amount of uncertainty—resisting quick judgement—he is able to stand back and listen to other voices more openly. Yet what is more fascinating to me is the way that taking a "stand on the issue" for Michael is linked to how he constructs an identity. As he put it, "I don't know who I am *yet*." In the essay, the writer discovers a self along with an argument, or makes it possible to "think oneself and thus create oneself" (Tetel 2). This is something that Michael senses intuitively. It is that self—or its *presence*, as I've termed it—that shapes and is shaped by the open inquiry.

For Michael, this is both exciting and unsettling. Free to explore his topic rather than to explain "what was in concrete before the beginning," he found the writing more honest, and more "natural" to write and to read. But his most significant discovery was to recognize the part that writing can play in leading him to meaning, rather than serving simply as an objective vehicle for transmitting fact. In contrast to past papers, Michael observes that "in this case, the writing led itself. . . . What I would write at one point would dictate the next part to be written." He is most eloquent about the generative power of language as he describes revision of his essay. Before he began the rewrite, he reflected on his instructor's comments. She urged Michael to keep "digging" at what seemed to be the central theme of his paper.

> I wonder if what she was trying to say in a very nice way was, yeah, but so what? What do you really mean? And I think that was the other thing I was really trying to dig at . . . I finally found my north star as it was . . . but *I had to dig through my own writing to get at it*, which was rather different. It's something I'd never experienced before. (emphasis added)

Michael's "north star," the force that guided him to what he wanted to say, was his own writing; it was an experience with which he was already familiar from writing essays earlier in the semester, but one that he had never before recognized was relevant when writing a research paper. For Michael, at least, the essayistic approach to research seemed to encourage an understanding of the power of language to construct reality rather than objectively transmit information about a reality discovered before it is described in words.[4]

Research and a Narrative of Thought

There are also some unsettling implications to the way the research essay makes the appropriation of knowledge personal. By unmasking the knower, the essay forces him to take responsibility for his judgements. At first, both Carrie and Michael responded to this in similar ways: They took refuge in the characterization of their essays as "I feel" papers. Sensing that this informal approach to research largely freed them from making authoritative statements that imply certainty or universality, they both concluded that their papers did not deal in "fact" but "just opinion." For a subjectivist like Carrie, the implication was that her claims were her own, not subject to debate because she doesn't pretend they represent some general truth: "Everyone can have an opinion. No one's opinion is wrong. So I don't think they should be able to judge the paper because they don't think it's right." At first, Michael had a somewhat similar view, but for him it was more an issue of honesty: "I didn't want to state something that could be argued is my opinion and make it sound like fact. I think it's almost deceiving the reader."

It appears that, in some ways, the research essay lets students off the hook. Because it seems to deal in opinion, not truth, students may feel less compelled to make defensible claims. I do worry about this, which is one reason why I'm spending more time in class these days unpacking terms like *opinion, fact,* and *truth* with students (see the next chapter), and raising questions that get at their epistemological beliefs. I want them to consider that an *opinion* is a kind of claim—much like a *fact* is—that should be supportable. But I also want them to see a new possibility in the research essay that is less available in the research paper: the opportunity to *test* an opinion or an idea to determine its truth.

Because the essay foregrounds the process of acquiring knowledge—*how* we come to know—it can be used to tell the story of how a writer arrives at an opinion or an understanding or an idea about her topic. A student who writes an essay on "Deep Blue," the IBM computer that defeated Russian chess champion Gary Kasporov, describes how his research began because of a chance encounter with a *Popular Science* article. He wonders, "So what is Deep Blue? A robot computer that learns, contemplates, and finds the correct chess moves on its own? Or a megacomputer that only can computer what is previously programmed into it? That was what I wanted to know." The student then tells the story of what he discovered as he researched this question. Another student who had a rash of bad dreams "just had to find out" whether there was something wrong with her. "I wanted to know if dreams could tell you specifics about a person," she writes, "and if certain characteristics in dreams mean anything that I should become aware of. . . . Soon my load of books from the library swelled, causing me to have nightmares of being engulfed among pages of print. . . . Here is what I discovered."

When these essays not only provide an account of where the student looked to discover the answers to the questions he poses—a narrative in the tradition of Macrorie's "I-Search" paper—but also include the story of how the writer's thinking evolved with each encounter with new information—a narrative of thought—then "opinions" are not simply "stuck in" or represented as mere expression of feeling. They are offered as integral products of the inquiry, attached to the evidence that both led to those opinions and perhaps complicated them. What I most love to see in research essays are moments when the writers turn the writing back on itself—"At first I believed this, and then I thought this, but now I've come to understand it this way." It is a move we recognize in the best personal essays, and it is one we can also encourage in the essayed research paper.

The Essay's Lessons Remain

Even when research essay doesn't work in these ways, I hope at the very least that it establishes curiosity as the force behind inquiry. Encouraged to see the world as the essayist does—uncertain, confusing, a "gigantic puzzle"—and given fairly free rein to find some piece of it to explore, students have a chance to recover the sense of wonder many lost somewhere along the way. It is "a mode of inquiry" students need to learn that the conventional term paper cannot provide, says composition theorist Chris Anderson: "Answers, abstractions, assertions come later, with experience and knowledge. Students first need to learn the discipline of exploring, of asking questions, of testing possibilities" (331). After using Lewis Thomas's essays in a composition course on research writing, Anderson confesses he was initially ambivalent about encouraging students to model such reflective writing. While the essays provided a provocative alternative to the more systematic and impersonal academic article, he feared he was letting down his students and his colleagues in other disciplines by not spending more time teaching the term paper. Ultimately, however, teaching the essay led him to "question again the subordination of the English Department to the practical demands of other disciplines."

> Yes, we have an obligation to teach our students how to write in the ways they will need to in other classes and out in the world, yet the implicit argument of Thomas's work is that we also have an obligation to teach how to discover and test who they are in the process of writing. . . . Even more than that, Thomas forces us to question the basic premises of those practical demands from other disciplines. If scientific research must proceed by error, motivated always by wonder, a sense of mystery, ground always in the sensibilities of the inquiring subject [as Thomas suggests], then the term paper as it is conventionally conceived is simply not useful, in any discipline. In both the form and the themes of his essays, Thomas argues that there are no easy answers, in any field, that everything must be seen in terms of the self, that every self must be in constant interaction with other things in the world and other people, that writing is relationship and that all good writing captures the act of relating, the process of thinking about important things. (330–1)

When it's successful, the research essay encourages students to own their words and the insights they glean from following those words. And just as it revives the notion of authorship effaced by the objective report of the conventional term paper, it strengthens the rhetorical relationship between writer and reader. As my students become writers who research, rather than researchers who have to write, I hope they expand the role they claimed earlier in the course as writers of personal essays. I hope they will come to share Richard Larson's observation that research is not a separate activity, "but can inform virtually any writing or speaking if the author wishes it to do so" (813). Accepting this, students can roam more widely, exploring questions through writing that they would have ignored earlier in the course because they run outside the range of their personal knowledge.

Rather than a separate activity, research becomes another source of information that helps students find out what they want to know, topics that remain deeply embedded in questions about who they are. Tim, a senior history major at the time I talked to him, told me that his experience with writing personal essays and a research paper in Freshman English that was "personally linked" was transformative for him, largely because it taught him to examine his own subjectivity, and particularly how the personal informs academic writing, even when he's not talking about himself.

> I think the key to being a good writer is that you have to know yourself. I think all good writing is a reflection of you, your way of looking at the world. . . . [I]f I go back and look at history papers over the years, I can see an improvement as I became more aware of myself. Your ability to think improves with that. While you might not talk about yourself in a paper, you know your views a little more. . . . Even with history papers, the connection is there. . . . If I hadn't kept a journal, and I hadn't had the opportunity in one class to write my thoughts, then my research papers would be rather blah. *I wouldn't know how to figure out what I think.* (Lippold, emphasis added)

The research essay makes "figuring out what I think" its subject, and in doing so, gives students like Tim a method for working out the relationship between the self and the world. And by giving students the confidence to project their voices into the Burkean parlor, they are more likely to keep the conversation going, and perhaps even to dissent from time to time. "I wrote plenty of those scientific papers where you label the introduction, the conclusion, you label the hypothesis," said Kate Carter, a senior in wildlife management. "But for me what was helpful is believing in my voice, not knowing I can write a scientific paper. . . . As the years went on, I think I would stray from the traditional format, including my voice and including opinions that weren't 'scientific.'. . . It ended up helping my paper."

As students like Kate and Tim progressively acquire the disciplinary habits of their respective fields, the essayist's sensibilities may be supplanted by those of a specialist. This is, in part, what a modern university education is supposed to do. But as both students demonstrate, the essay's lessons remain.

Notes

1. In "On Experience," which is Montaigne's most eloquent and complete statement of his beliefs, he complains that "there are more books on books than any other subject" and "there is more trouble interpreting interpretations than in interpreting the things themselves." This could be a critique of modern scholarship, which has made its business, as Montaigne put it, "learning to understand the learned" rather than reporting first-hand encounters with the objects of study.

2. Moffett also argues that the movement from "narrative discourse" to "explicit generalization"—or in our students' papers, from showing to telling, or exposition to anecdote, and so on—"necessarily entails shifts in language and rhetoric" that involve "different language structures and compositional issues" (53). Among these are grammatical shifts, including tense, transitions, and organization, as well as paragraph structure. That may account for the frequent student—and instructor—complaint that when writing a researched essay, they don't like the shift in tone between the expository and narrative parts.

3. In a study of graduate students' efforts to rewrite their highly technical papers for a lay audience, David Green reports that one of his subjects "felt that writing nontechnically allowed him to express conviction" (375). While Green's study didn't assert that this was true of all the students he studied, I would maintain that it describes the feelings of many of my students who are encouraged to approach the research paper informally.

4. The research essay's form contributes to students' discovery of the constitutive nature of language, but so does its emphasis on "unpacking" sometimes technical language for a more general audience. Green's study of the writing of graduate students in psychology demonstrated that when they were asked to rewrite their technical prose to clarify its meaning for a nontechnical audience, the students found that the writing gave them a new understanding of their research problem. As Green put it, they discovered that "writing becomes a resource for discovery and the page a type of laboratory." (378)

Four

Skating Backwards on Thin Ice
Teaching the Research Essay

Six hundred years ago, the patron saint of ice skating fell on the ice and broke her ribs. She never fully recovered, and spent the rest of her life in prayer. I'm not sure why ice skating rated a patron saint, except that it is one of those things—like losing a wallet—that sometimes inspires prayer. I consider this fact as I glide along the frozen Lamprey River, near my New Hampshire home, and listen to the thump and ping of shifting ice.

I try to trust the physics of frozen water. My friend Brock tells me that two inches of ice will easily hold a person, and that the four inches below my blades make skating completely safe. My yellow lab doesn't buy any of it, and she trails us from the bank, whining whenever she is forced to cross the frozen river. When it groans from our weight, she tucks her tail between her legs and races back to solid ground.

There is something to be said for instinct.

I have skated often this winter. The cold, snowless days have stretched in January, and on the ponds a cap of ice—like the paraffin on a jelly jar—safely seals the black water below. Even the rivers like the Lamprey, where moving water normally resists ice, are frozen to the dams and to the edge of the heaviest rapids. Like Dutch canals, the rivers wind their way through the New Hampshire countryside.

Ice travel is new to me. Though I grew up skating, it was mostly on a flooded playground, where people skated in large, slow circles to music that came from metal speakers high on telephone poles. Skating was a social activity, one of the few during the seventh grade in which it was possible not only to talk to girls, but to touch them. I was always somewhere nearby when Lori Jo Flink lost her balance.

I don't remember the day I first learned to skate backwards, which surprises me now, because I do remember the day I did my first back-flip off a diving board. Both are ways that I marked my passage through those awkward years. I would begin on one end of the skating rink and begin wiggling my way backwards to the other end, watching the undulating trail my blades etched on the ice, not daring to look behind me to see if I were about to smash into the low wooden wall of the adjacent hockey rink. It was one of the first times I felt I had mastered something physical, something involving the choreography of feet, legs, hips, and arms. I imagined I was very good at skating backwards. I imagined that Lori Jo knew it, too.

This is the beginning to an essay I wrote several years ago, and it insists on making an appearance here. I'm not sure why. On second thought, there's an obvious reason, one that comes to mind almost immediately: Asking students to write essays, and *research* essays in particular, involves faith in thin ice. If a guiding principle of the Montaignian essay is that it is genuinely exploratory—it sets out to find out rather than to prove—then to teach the essay demands that we convince our students to go against their instinct to rush to judgement. Uncertainty is uncomfortable, and it certainly runs counter to their training in school writing—especially the conventional research paper—with its emphasis on mastering formal conventions and accumulating evidence to make a point. Even students who do, initially, dare to approach their subjects openly may head for the bank at the first sound of shifting ice; it might be a teacher's critical comment, an encounter with a research source that seems to have all the answers, or the awkwardness of their own prose as it struggles towards meaning.

Just as Brock taught me to trust two inches of ice, to read the sounds of shifting ice not as signs of certain danger but as signs of my own movement over its uneven surface, composition instructors must find ways to teach the research essay as a journey across and into disciplines that, like the ice on the Lamprey, shift and grind against each other.

But how are we to do this? And if we encourage students to explore rather than prove, don't we risk promoting a discourse that is not only a poor model of traditional academic writing, but also poor writing as well—unfocused, digressive, pointless? In this chapter, I examine some practical considerations of teaching the research essay, including the questions I raise here. While students like Michael seem to easily embrace the essay genre as a means of finding new meaning and a new approach to researched topics, the struggles of students like Carrie are much more typical. Urged to explore, they revert to proving what they already know. Encouraged to express themselves, they look for places to "stick in" their opinions. Asked to be Hucks, they are more comfortable being Toms. How can we teach the research essay to these students so that they, too, learn to exploit its possibilities?

I realize now that there is another reason I chose to begin this chapter with the opening of my own unfinished personal essay. It is an essayistic intrusion into a text that has seemed to lose that quality in the last three chapters. I did not know what would happen if I began the chapter this way, but I trusted that somehow, by jamming the frequency of the argument I've been making up until now with a personal digression, something interesting would happen. And something did. I found a metaphor that helped me explain what I want to do in this chapter, and deepened my own understanding of the challenges my students face when they do what I am asking them to do here: write researched essays instead of term papers.

I recall now what prompted the essay on ice skating. A winter of no snow left the river with clear ice for months—a remarkable occurrence—and I skated as much as I could. The more I skated, the more I reflected on skating; I began attending to the experience in a writerly way. I wondered about the physics of ice—what's so magical about two inches? I wondered about skating accidents, about people who misread the ice. I wondered about skating Dutch canals, and what the skaters used before steel blades. All of these questions took me to the library, where I discovered, among other things, the patron saint of ice skating and sketches of Dutchmen skating on bones. But along with *wondering*, I also *remembered*: the sensation of skating backwards, the smell of wet rubber mats in the warming house, and, of course, Lori Jo Flink. There is in this wondering and remembering—questioning and self-reflecting—a looking outward and inward that is exactly what we are trying to teach when we teach the research essay. It is now habit with me. But how do we teach it to our students, most of whom don't share the habit? How do we help them to see how experience can easily yield researchable questions? How do we help them see how experience can deepen their understanding of what they find in their research, as it has for me here, and learn to integrate personal knowledge with worldly knowledge so that they achieve the "new way of thinking" Belenky and co-authors describe as characteristic of "constructivist" knowing (134), or as one of their subjects put it, to learn to "let the inside out and the outside in" (135)?

These are difficult questions, but in this chapter I elaborate on a practical pedagogy that encourages students to see personal experience and knowledge as a means of moving outward into the world, and language as a vehicle for negotiating the journey. I also suggest ways to encourage students to see research the way Chris Anderson believes Lewis Thomas does: "motivated always by wonder, a sense of mystery, [and] ground in the sensibilities of the inquiring subject" (331). This spirit of inquiry demands, of course, something that is very difficult to teach: a willingness to put up with doubt, and a faith that skating backwards on thin ice is worth the risk of running into a wooden wall. As Ann Berthoff reminds us, however, there are certain "essential acts of mind" that should be embedded in the first assignment we give that are also present in the last, and a tolerance of ambiguity and a willingness to suspend judgement are among them. How do we help our students apply these habits of mind to an assignment they have always considered closed rather than open-ended? How do we help them draw on what they've already learned about writing and inquiry from their essays earlier in the semester?

For writing teachers who spend the semester cultivating a "writing community" in their classrooms, the research assignment can seem to poison the village well. It's not simply that many students dislike research. They often respond to the assignment by assuming a role that is sharply at odds with the one teachers have been trying to cultivate: Students don't see themselves as "authors" but actors in someone else's script. They become passive rather than purposeful. "How many pages is this supposed to be?" they inevitably ask. They return to their previous view of writing as mechanical rather than generative; they surrender their earlier commitments to exploratory writing, invention, and revision, and postpone any kind of writing until the last possible moment, and then its purpose is not to think things through but simply get things down. In short, as Richard Larson pointed out, students see research as a wholly "separate activity" ("The 'Research Paper'" 814) with little or no relation to the other work they've done as writers in the composition class.

A curriculum to teach the research *essay* would offer the assignment not as something to taint the well and drive the villagers back into their huts, but rather as simply an extension of the commons, a place where a community of writers extends its reach beyond the voices in the classroom to others who speak at its margins. Rather than abandoning their roles as writers, students see research as something that adds to the practices they've already developed while writing essays all semester. They are writers who research, rather than researchers who have to write. But how do we do this?

Redefining Research

"I've always wondered about dog food," begins Ann Hodgman in her essay, "No Wonder They Call Me a Bitch." She wonders, among other things, whether Gainesburgers are really burgers, and whether Gravy

Train delivers on its promise to make gravy. "And exactly what *are* by-products?" Hodgman asks in the final line of her lead paragraph (112)."

"Having spent the better part of a week eating dog food," Hodgman suddenly tell us, "I'm sorry to say that I now know the answers to these questions." Hodgman's piece, which appeared some years back in *Spy Magazine* and later in *Best American Essays,* goes on to detail, as you can probably guess, how she dined on "stinky, white-flecked mush" and "stinky fat-drenched nuggets," all of which failed to deliver on their advertising promises. At first, it's an essay that seems miles away from academic research, one that has no place, certainly, in a college writing course. That may be why "No Wonder They Call Me a Bitch" is so effective as an opening blow against students' assumptions about research. Hodgman *is* a researcher. Her project is driven by questions, not answers. She uses a range of sources of information to explore the topic—she interviews pet food company spokespeople, studies their advertising claims, and makes field observations. And at the heart of her humorous treatment of the topic, Hodgman has a serious point: The selling of dog food to appeal to human sensibilities is absurd. Sure, her essay is not a model of formal academic research in many other ways, but as an introduction to the spirit of inquiry, "No Wonder They Call Me a Bitch" is a pedagogical gem.

Teaching the research essay must begin by challenging some of the "rules" of research writing students assume are already scripted: that they must be "objective," make original contributions to knowledge, follow a strict format, always have a thesis before they start, write for a specialized audience, and choose topics that are removed from their "everyday life."[1] What they seem to believe most of all is that "facts" poison prose; any writing that deploys research has got to be dull, dull, dull. Of course part of this attitude comes from a simple misunderstanding about the nature of specialized discourses. Composition students are still outsiders to the particular conventions and ways of thinking that are reflected in the often dense, difficult prose of academic journals and books. But this explanation has little power for the freshman researcher, poised to undertake her first college research paper. That's why lively researched essays, like Hodgman's, offer such a powerful alternative to students ready to believe that fact-based writing has to be mind-numbing.[2] Such examples of compelling fact-based writing abound. Among the essayists, the work of Barry Lopez, Diane Ackerman, John McPhee, David Quammen, Nancy Mairs, and Annie Dillard offer wonderful models. So does the writing of countless creative nonfiction writers whose work appears in magazines such as *Natural History, The New Yorker, Smithsonian, Mother Jones,* or *Audubon.* But even some academic essays offer students a surprising departure from the expected, and these might also be used in a writing class emphasizing the research essay.

Academic discourse, as David Bartholomae pointed out, is "one thing only in convenient arguments" ("Writing" 62). There are many academic discourses, and some represent clear departures from the scientific model that historically dominated scholarship, including published work in the sciences. Speaking of canines, M. Dane Picard, for example, begins his article in the *Journal of Geological Education* with an anecdote about his dog.

> One late afternoon early in June, long after all the deer had moved
> off the mountain flank to summer grazing on mountain meadows,
> a young muley doe ran up the slope south of the Russian olives
> and passed within a few feet of where I was sitting on faulted
> Traissic limestone. There had been no herds of deer on the moun-
> tain flank since early in May. (542)

The piece goes on to explore theories that the strange behavior of animals can help predict earthquakes.

Those of us in English studies recognize such personal or autobiographical scholarship—or research that essays rather than argues—as increasingly common, but it is a strand in the scholarship in many academic fields.[3] As a way to broaden their notions of academic research beyond the dominant scientific model, I think it's useful to share such alternative scholarship with our students as they are about to embark on their own projects. However, the best models for inspiring students to rethink what it means to do research and consider how they might approach their own projects are essays like "No Wonder They Call Me a Bitch," creative nonfiction works that are carefully researched and focused, yet written with an engaging voice.

Topics in the "Everyday World"

For some years, I've been using an essay by Richard Conniff, a science writer who often publishes in magazines such as *Audubon* and *Discovery*. "Why Did God Make Flies" is very much written in the essay tradition—it is subjective, digressive, and concerned with the ordinary. What could be more ordinary than the housefly, the subject of Conniff's meditation? Why *did* God create them? One of the first things essays like this can teach is that the essayist is fascinated by the commonplace. "The world is everywhere whispering essays" (460), wrote the nineteenth-century British essayist Alexander Smith, and it is this celebration of wide availability of subject matter for the researched essay that is exemplified by the work of Diane Ackerman, Conniff, Lewis Thomas, John McPhee, Barry Lopez, David Quammen, Nancy Mairs, and others. For example, one can write powerfully on houseflies, as Conniff does; on oranges, as McPhee does; on kissing, one of my favorite Ackerman topics; and on multiple sclerosis, Mairs' affliction. To help our students see the promise of their often ordinary experiences as material for the research essay, we must ask them this question: What have you seen or experienced that raises questions that research can help to answer?

This connection between inquiry and the "everyday world" is wonderfully illustrated by Conniff's essay, which begins by revealing the situation that gave rise to the question that prompted his research.

> A fly is standing on the rim of my beer glass as I write these words. Its vast, mosaic eyes look simultaneously lifeless and mocking. It grooms itself methodically, its forelegs entwining like the arms of a Sybarite luxuriating in bath oil. Its hind legs twitch across the upper surface of its wings. It pauses, well fed and at rest, to contemplate the sweetness of life. . . . With the possible exception of *Homo sapiens*, it is hard to imagine an animal as disgusting or improbable as the housefly. No bestiary concocted from the nightmares of the medieval mind could have come up with such a fantastic animal. If we went to study nature in its most exotic permutations the best place is to begin here, at home, on the rim of my beer glass. (9–10, 11)

An ordinary encounter with a fly on a beer glass—one that will seem familiar to many of us—begins Conniff's investigation. Unfortunately, our students rarely see the possibility of everyday observations as a source of wonder, and certainly not as a source of topics for a research essay. But if they've had the experience in autobiographical writing of finding that even the most commonplace events can be charged with meaning, then they are likely to accept that their experiences can also yield interesting questions that research might help answer. A student who aspires to be an actor wonders how skilled performers can cry on command; she launches an investigation on method acting. Another student who recently attended an Irish wake wonders about the purpose of its "strange" rituals; she explores its historical basis in a research project. An older student comes to composition class after meeting about his son with local school officials, who recommend medication for treatment of attention deficit disorder (ADD); the student researches methods of diagnosing ADD. Why do we need sleep? That was an obvious question for a college student fresh from a series of all-nighters. Her research essay, "The Pull of Sleep," explores the question. All of these topics arise from the students' experiences or observations. Some of them could have easily been topics for personal essays, but when they are cast as research topics, they take the writers beyond the village boundaries.

But we must remind them of what they learned writing their personal narratives in E 101: that what makes an experience interesting to explore is not what you already know about it but what you want to find out. At the heart of inquiry—and essay writing, for that matter—is finding the questions that make even the most mundane topics come to life.

Seeing the World Through Questions

What *was* that fly doing on Conniff's beer glass? (To be brief, "puking and preening.") What are the "poultry by-products" which are so often listed as an ingredient in pet food? (According to Hodgman, "necks, intestines, undeveloped eggs and other 'carcass remnants.'") Is it true that animals behave strangely before an earthquake? (There is, as yet, no convincing scientific proof, but the Chinese believe it.) When did kissing begin? (It may have started, says Ackerman, from the habit of getting close to someone to inhale their scent.) What all of these writers share is a delightful penchant for looking at the everyday world and seeing questions, and through questions, they "estrange the familiar," as Douglas Atkins puts it. There is no boring topic—only uninteresting questions.

We can teach this to our students most dramatically when we ask them to do the same things these essayists did: Imagine questions that make the familiar new. This is easier than it sounds, partly because they've been doing it all along. As students write essays in E 101, they discover that the more they look at a subject, the more they see, even if it's something they've seen before. They often first discover this when they write about an experience that they think they know well. Questions frequently figure into this re-vision: What do I understand about this now that I didn't then? What surprised me? What difference did it make that this happened? Students can extend the heuristic power of questions to help them reflect on things outside of themselves as well, to inquire as an essayist "who turns his object this way and that, who questions it, feels it, tests it, thoroughly reflects on it, attacks it from different angles" (Bense, quoted in Adorno 164). The following exercise will introduce students to what that can mean.

Classroom Exercise: The Myth of the Boring Topic

- Organize students in small groups. Provide each group with two things: a sheet of newsprint and a commonplace object. Consider things like a pencil, a can of dog food, an orange, a paperclip, a shoe, or a floppy disk. Give each group a different object.
- Challenge each group to brainstorm a list of potentially interesting questions about their objects. They should list the questions on their newsprint, which will later be posted on the wall.

- After twenty minutes or so, each group physically moves to the adjacent group's newsprint, examining the object and the questions before them. They are now charged with adding a few more questions that the group before them didn't consider. This activity need not take much longer than five minutes.

- Next, ask each group to separately discuss the long list of questions that have, by now, been generated about the pencil or the orange or the shoe or whatever familiar object you've chosen for the exercise. Group members must now agree which *one* question they find most interesting about their mundane object, and second, which question on the list might be most "researchable"; that is, if they were an editorial team assigned to propose a re-searched article for a general interest magazine that focused on their object, what might be the starting question for the investigation? The most interesting question and the most researchable question may or may not be the same. Ask the group to circle the questions they've chosen and post the newsprint on the wall for everyone in the class to see.

One of the first things you'll notice as the groups generate questions is how silly the questions can be. The exercise invites play, not a bad thing to encourage to counter the somberness that is usually associated with a research assignment, and it is through such play that students quickly recognize how questions help them re-see their world, and even make something as mundane as a shoe or a paperclip worth thinking about, for at least a little while. But I also want to move students to see that certain questions make even the most ordinary things interesting, and that some questions are better than others as a starting place for research. This becomes apparent as the class discusses the circled questions from the last step in the exercise. For example, the group that circles the question "How do they get the lead inside a pencil?" as the most interesting one will rightly wonder whether a whole essay could investigate such a query. At the same time, asking "Who invented shoes?" seems overly ambitious.

I like the discussion about what is a "researchable" question, and I'll often help it along by asking each group to examine their newsprint lists for certain *categories* of questions about their object. Do some questions seem to group together in a logical way? Are some questions, for example, about the *process* of creating or making their object? Are some *historical*? Do some deal with current social or cultural *trends* or the possible *uses* of the object? As groups begin to organize the random questions on their newsprint into categories, it becomes easier for students to imagine *types* of research projects—and the questions that seem to cluster around them—on, say, a pencil or a paperclip that might be feasible, even for them. A group proposing a project on an orange might choose to examine its historical origins, and easily generate questions—such as "From what region in the world did the orange originate?" and "How did it figure in the diet of early Americans?"—that are reasonable openings for a research essay.

I am pleased when this exercise reminds my students that material for writing—even a research paper—is everywhere, and that inquiry is driven not by answers but by questions. I want them to see that writing to learn applies to the research essay just as it applied to the personal narrative. But what I am really hoping for is a revival of curiosity as a motive for research. Not just any question that arises from personal experience or personal interest will do; it must be a question to which there is no quick answer, for as Dewey points out, curiosity becomes *intellectual* when "its ends are more remote." He writes,

> To the degree that a distant end controls a sequence of inquiries
> and observations and binds them together as a means to an end,
> just to that degree does curiosity assume a definite intellectual
> character. (39)

That "distant end" for the essayist is to discover how the personal context that gave rise to the question might be changed by the answers she discovers along the way. Those discoveries must be measured constantly against the writer's perceptions, personal knowledge, and intuition, but they also should be complicated by many other voices and perspectives. Research questions that are easy to answer, or do not lead students to encounters with multiple perspectives, are not as productive. As I reflect, for example, on Carrie's research on *The Simpson's*, I wonder if another reason her essay seemed to revert to a more conventional thesis-example approach was her inability to find conflicting views or sources other than popular magazines. Had she confronted more authoritative sources—particularly journal articles or interviews with TV experts—that represented colliding points of view, Carrie might have had more to work out. Her topic choice, however, might have made that more difficult.

What some students like Carrie might fail to recognize at first are the new possibilities that "essaying" their research create, especially for topic choice. Freed from the need to always argue a point in their paper, students can explore any topic that they find puzzling in interesting ways. They need not know what they think or what they want to say before they start. That opens up considerably the range of possible topics. What subject do they want to learn about? What complicated issue do they want to explore? At the same time, essaying rather than arguing can fundamentally shift students' terms of engagement with outside sources and knowledge. They are free to adopt, as Michael put

Table 4–1. The Dialectical Habit of Mind

Mountain of reflection	←→	Sea of experience
Ideas about	←→	Observations of
Telling	←→	Showing
Now	←→	Then
Generalities	←→	Specifics
What happens	←→	What Happened
Focusing	←→	Collecting
Order	←→	Chaos
Judging	←→	Playing
Theories	←→	Evidence
Criticizing	←→	Generating

it, a "beginner's mind," a stance that makes them more open to conflicting points of view, and less likely to dismiss voices with which they may not agree. Students may even be willing to ask questions that complicate their understanding of a topic; they are certainly more willing to engage in a *conversation* with sources in their attempt to work things out.

Teaching the Dialectics of Research

What the research essay can do that the research paper can't is shift students' roles as researchers. They are jolted out of a passive role and become much more active agents in the negotiation about what might be true. That discovery of new meanings or new ways of seeing can emerge from writing shouldn't be a revelation to our students by the time they begin the research assignment; they've already likely had at least a few surprises writing essays, perhaps especially personal narratives. They've practiced the negotiation of meaning in interpreting their own experiences. What they may not have done much is apply that same dialectic to figuring out what they think about a topic they know less well and placing their voices next to the voices of others.

One way, then, to help students bridge the "abyss" between essay writing and research writing is to remind them that they have already cultivated the dialectical habit of mind. They just need to apply it to a new and somewhat more complicated writing task. For example, in the personal narrative they have already practiced moving from *showing* and *telling* and back again (Table 4–1). This is not just a stylistic move, but an intellectual one. It involves abstracting from their experiences some ideas about what they might mean, a movement back and forth between what happened and what happens or the observations of things and their ideas about them. It is an act of looking at the evidence they have collected from their experiences and suggesting some theories that might explain their significance. This movement also implies a process and a certain stance the writer–researcher adopts towards her subject. At times she simply generates material or collects information, suspending judgement. At other moments she examines it critically, even cooly, attempting to make judgments. This dialectical practice is, of course, at the heart of academic inquiry, just as it is central to most writing process classrooms. But how do we help students apply it to the more complex task of writing with sources rather than writing just about their own experiences?

I think it might begin with the first reading assignments in E 101, those initial encounters our students have with other voices and other views. How do we structure these encounters? In particular, how can we encourage students to approach them dialectically, moving back and forth between experiencing the particulars in the text and reflecting on what they might suggest about an author's purpose and the reader's own sense of what might be true? Ann Berthoff's "double- entry journal," or similar methods that encourage students to engage in dialectical practice as they read, can get students started early in a writing course practicing the kind of writing and thinking that will be invaluable when they get to the research assignment. I frequently introduce the method in the first few weeks of class and encourage students to use it for a range of activities throughout the course—not just for responding to readings, but for use in collecting and interpreting field observations and even interview material. But I certainly encourage students to use dialectical note taking during the middle of the research process (see Appendix B, "Teaching the Double-Entry (or Dialogue) Journal"), a time when most composition texts have little to say about writing, unless, of course, they're instructing students about note cards.

"Essaying" Notes

Though note cards may be the symbol of student frustration with what they perceive is the meaninglessness of the research assignment and the failure of many of us to teach it well, I believe that note taking also represents a moment in the research process that may be the key to its success. In preceding chapters I argued that, for many students, difficulties with research writing often were related to epistemological beliefs, and particularly the struggle to develop a faith in one's ability to speak with authority about knowledge outside the self, territory that is already staked out by experts. I have come to believe that it is in the *middle* of the research process—the so-called note-taking stage—where these negotiations might take place most productively for the student writer. For many students (and instructors less comfortable with the digressive and tentative quality of the essay), it may be the note-taking stage, not the drafting stage, when the exploratory writing I'm promoting here makes the most sense.

As Doug Brent points out in *Reading as Rhetorical Invention*, composition texts have been strangely silent on how students "perform the intricate rhetorical dance" of reading and evaluating sources: "[I]nstruction on the research process . . . deals with the beginning and the end of the process (using the library and writing the drafts), but it has a gaping hole in the middle where much of the real work of knowledge construction is performed" (105). Since the research paper was introduced into Freshman Composition in the 1920s, that hole has been mostly filled with talk about note cards. While note cards have their merits, they have generally reinforced the idea that research is not about the construction of knowledge, but the collection of it.

Then what can we talk about beyond note cards? For many years, I had very little to say. Disdainful of note cards because of my own high school experience, I couldn't bring myself to say much about how to take notes for a research paper. Instead, I would refer my students to appropriate sections in our textbook, if we were using one, which would usually include the obligatory section on what to write where on an index card, and feature exhaustive explanations of what is meant by *summary, quotation,* and *paraphrase.* I noticed that a few students dutifully used note cards as they researched their freshman research papers, but most did not. What did they do instead? They photocopied to beat the band.

The omnipresence of the photocopy machine in the college library—and now the ease of downloading documents from the Internet—have fundamentally changed information gathering for students. They take fewer notes, and I think there may be some profound implications to this. What does it mean that students delay writing about and with their sources until they begin a draft? How does that delay affect their own position of authority as they seek ways to use their sources? How does it affect the ways students express themselves?

As I've noted before, students often have great difficulty incorporating outside texts into their own writing. The seams show everywhere, and they can be particularly evident in the research essay. For example, students may adopt stiff, often pedantic language, or create an obvious shift in tone between informational passages and more personal ones, or completely surrender to the words and ideas of outside authorities by using long, quoted passages. In the worst cases, students commit (usually unintentional) plagiarism. The challenge for our students, suggests Bahktin, is that they must "populate" alien discourses "with (their) own intentions," something he concedes is "a difficult and complicated process" (293–4). The research essay highlights this struggle, I believe, because of the genre's explicit subjectivity and contextuality—the essay must be "populated" by the writer's intentions and foreground the context from which the research question arises, or it is not an essay. Students can get around this to some extent by avoiding difficult texts, as Carrie did in her essay on *The Simpson's*; popular periodicals and books often represent discourses (and views, in this case) that are not so alien, and therefore more easily appropriated. But even then, the seams often show.

This is a struggle not only over the possession of words, but also over authority—who will control the discourse—the student or her sources? I've already suggested that the "essayistic" alternative to traditional research paper instruction seems to grant students more authority, but Bahktin offers a further insight: The appropriation of other discourses is more or less complicated based on their distance from what he calls "the zone of contact" (345). It is the contact zone where two different discourses encounter each other, each competing for authority, when an "authoritative discourse" no longer has its usual distance from the speaker (or writer's) own "internally persuasive discourse" (342), something I would roughly equate with "voice."[4] Put more simply, when it is drawn into the zone of contact, authoritative discourse is more approachable, less reified, and therefore easier to consider dialectically. I believe that the moment this is most likely to occur for many student researchers may not be the drafting stage, when they are confronting a whole array of other writing problems (purpose, structure, documentation, coherence, etc.). Instead, authoritative discourse is more likely to be drawn into the zone of contact when they first encounter it, at the note-taking stage, in the middle of the research process as they're reading (or interviewing or observing) for their paper. Note taking, then, becomes more than a mechanical process of vacuuming up information to deposit later; instead, it becomes a key site for the negotiation of authority in their papers.

If this is true, conventional note cards will simply not do. They are just not big enough for the messy and, in some cases, extensive writing that students might generate as they struggle to take possession of other peoples' words. On the other hand, the double-entry journal, or some other note-taking method that encourages students to constantly move back and forth between what they're reading and what they think about what they're reading, helps many of my students see their encounters with sources as occasions for *conversation*, not monologue. This idea is obviously at the heart of the dialectical note taking. But it can be made even clearer to students by using a variation on an exercise suggested by Paul Heilker in his book *The Essay: Theory and Pedagogy for an Active Form*.

Heilker observes that students' resistance to writing essays is often linked to the "heretical" notion that school writing *can* be written in the first person and openly subjective. "The best way through this resistance," he writes, "is to present my students with a widely used metaphor for the essay: I suggest that they conceive of the essay as a 'conversation' the writer has with her sources and herself" (100).

Heilker begins by collaborating with his students on generating a list of words they associate with the word *conversation*. Whenever I've done this, the list builds quickly on the blackboard, and it includes such words as *intimate, humor, digressive, listening, arguing, agreeing, disagreeing, questioning*, and so on. Heilker then tells his students to imagine they are about to have a conversation over lunch with the author of the quoted passage he is about to share, and that they are to respond in writing, remembering some of the qualities of conversation they listed on the board. He then provides them with a provocative quotation, usually only a line or two, and students compose a one-paragraph response, representing their effort to "continue the conversation" (101).

I love this exercise, but wanted to expand and extend it as an introduction to double-entry note taking. Instead of a short quotation, I use a slightly longer one, and then introduce—in sequence—two additional quotations from the same author. It helps, I think, to choose quotations that are provocative, passages that are likely to engage students and inspire them to *talk back* and *talk with*. In the following exercise, I chose to excerpt an article by University of Virginia professor Mark Edmundson (1997) in the *Harper's*, which, among other things, takes contemporary American universities—and by implication, contemporary students—to task for creating a "culture of consumption and entertainment," where campus funds go to building new rec centers rather than improving curriculum. My students *do* want to talk with Edmundson about his ideas.

Classroom Exercise: Getting a Word in Edgewise

- Explain to your students that they are about to have an imaginary lunch with someone named Mark Edmundson, who in between bites of his BLT suddenly blurts out, "I've got something on my mind, and I just have to share it with you!" Then share with the entire class (on transparency or handout) the following quotation:

    Whether the students are sorority/fraternity types, grunge afficionados, piercer/tatooers, black or white, rich or middle class . . . , they are, nearly across the board, very, very self-contained. On good days they display a light, appealing glow; on bad days, shuffling disgruntlement. But there's little fire, little passion to be found. (41)

Encourage students to respond in a six- or seven-minute fast-write to Edmundson's comment, remembering the words they associated with *conversation*. Urge them to remember the setting and the situation for this imaginary conversation.

- Edmundson listens politely to what each of your students has to say to his first thought, but now he feels compelled to elaborate. He interrupts, and adds,

  > Before they arrive, we ply students with luscious ads, guaranteeing them a cross between summer camp and lotusland. When they get here, flattery and nonstop entertainment are available, if that's what they want. . . . Is it a surprise, then, that this generation of students—steeped in consumer culture before going off to school, treated as potent customers by the university well before their date of arrival, then pandered to from day one . . . are inclined to see the books they read as a string of entertainments to be placidly enjoyed or languidly cast down? (46–7)

Repeat the earlier instructions: Students are to take up the lunch table conversation again in another fastwrite, now considering what Edmundson has just shared.

- The BLT gone, the conversation flagging, Edmundson wipes his mouth with a paper napkin, and says, "I've got just one last thing to say about this. Hear me out, won't you?"

  > Perhaps it would be a good idea to try firing the counselors and sending half the deans back into their classrooms, dismantling the football team and making the stadium into a playground for local kids, emptying the fraternities, and boarding up the student-activities office. Such measures would convey the message that American colleges are not northern outposts of Club Med. (49)

Tell students to write one final response. As before, encourage them to write quickly, with the imaginary lunch table conversation in mind.

- Provide your students with the full text of the Edmundson article (or whatever reading you choose for the exercise), and tell them their assignment: Using the in-class fastwriting and Edmundson's text, they are to write an essay that explores some question their writing and reading inspired.

The in-class writing prompted by Mark Edmundson's piece is often fast and furious. The article gets a rise out of them, yet his argument is substantial enough that they can't simply dismiss it. Class discussion will obviously focus on the merits of his argument, but at some point I always try to turn talk towards the *experience* students had responding to this author. How did the open-ended and conversational written response influence the way they thought about the article? How did that thinking evolve *over time*? How did this kind of writing effect they way they *read* Edmundson? How might it effect any reading? How does this compare with more conventional note taking?

What I want students to see is how they have just practiced the kind of dialectical thinking that the double-entry journal encourages. If they imagine that the line down the middle of the page is a lunch table, and on the left are the ideas of an author and on the right are their responses to those ideas, then they might see the kinds of conversations that might take place *as* they do research. The conversations might not always be as spirited as this one. Sometimes it can focus on the writer's attempt to clarify what an author might be saying. Sometimes the writer tries, through writing, to extend or apply what an author is saying to the particular context of their research project. In addition, as Heilker points out, this conversation occurs *over time*. This "chrono-logic" is particularly apparent in the exercise, since there are three separate writing episodes, all of which will likely build on the one that came before it. The drama of a writer trying to work something out in a narrative of thought is an important quality of the essay, and so the exercise models the act of essaying as well. Here students can consider how they might use the essay as a mode of inquiry, *even if they're aim is to produce a conventional argumentative research paper*. Rather than "taking" notes, they can "essay" them.

Finally, how students manage to incorporate these notes and Edmundson's text in a short essay—placing their voices with his—gives them practice in negotiating between the personal and the expository, between private and public knowledge, which when successful, will help students close the seams in their research essays.

Narrative Thinking and the Research Essay

The thing about skating backwards is that you don't know where you're going, but you can see where you've been. When the ice is smooth and black, my steel blades finely etch its surface, and two white undulating lines stretch away from me until they disappear in the glare. I like these lines because they record my presence—it is *my* trail I'm etching on the ice—a presence that is both historical and immediate. I can see where I've been, but I can also see where I am any moment. The essay seems to reflect this way of seeing, I think, in its reluctance to anticipate where it's going, and its fascination with the self in motion—who was I, and who am I becoming? But the essayist's particular interest is much more immediate than historical. She asks, "Who am I, and what do I know *now*?"

There are several practical implications of this. One is the essayist's willingness to enact the drama of figuring out what she thinks in prose, much the way someone does it in conversation with a good friend. I am doing that right now, and I did it in the beginning of this chapter as I tried to explain, through second thoughts and third thoughts, why I began the chapter the way I did, what relevance ice skating on the Lamprey might have for this project. This demands a certain amount of faith: faith that the trail of words I'm making will lead somewhere, faith in the usefulness of digression, in undulating lines of thought rather than linear ones. I must also assume that the drama of working things out at the point of utterance is as interesting to a reader as it is to me.

I am describing here, I think, a particular mode of thinking that can be distinguished from analysis and argument not just by its lack of linearity or systematic method, but also by its concern with process, and, in particular, the positioning of thought in time and place: What do I know now under these circumstances? Now what do I think? And now? This is narrative thinking, a chronology of thought that stretches behind me like lines etched on black ice. Of course, narrative thinking is not held in very high esteem in the academy, but as Thomas Newkirk points out, the assignment of abstract and theoretical thinking as more valued than narrative thought is a hierarchy that, to some extent, reflects our own academic biases simply because it validates what we do (25).

I value narrative thinking—and want to teach it to my students through the essay—because it creates a trail of a mind in motion, dialogically engaged with itself and the object of inquiry, constantly doing and undoing claims about what seems true. This dialogue becomes richer with the research essay because it brings more voices into the conversation, *if* they are invited to unsettle as well as settle things. Quite understandably, my students are much more willing to do this in an exercise like the one I described earlier on the Edmundson piece— or during the note-taking phase—then they are in their drafts. The traditional research paper genre, which foregrounds authoritative conclusions rather than the process of coming up with them, is simply too powerful a model for some of my students to write against. So I celebrate their willingness to indulge in narrative thinking in the middle of the research process, even if they don't do it in their drafts.

In fact, telling themselves *the story* of how their thinking about their topics evolved before they begin the draft is often a means to move them towards a thesis. A "loop-writing" exercise[5] is often helpful.

Classroom Exercise: Looping Towards a Thesis

After your students have accumulated a critical mass of information on their topics—enough information that they begin to complain of being "swamped" or overwhelmed—ask them to review all their notes and reread all their published material before class. When they come to class, give them the following instructions:

- Tell your students to clear their desks of research materials, *except* for a journal or notebook in which to write. They are to write fast for five minutes without stopping, telling the *story* of their research. When they began the project, what were their preconceptions or assumptions about their topics? Then what happened? What happened after that? What do they think now? Encourage them, as they tell this story, to be honest with themselves and to admit things that still confuse them or ideas about which they still feel quite tentative. They may also account for their feelings about the topic as well as their ideas about it.

- Now prepare students for another five-minute fastwrite. This time, the prompt is "Moments, Stories, People, and Scenes." These might be specific case studies, people, situations, or personal observations that seem to figure in their narrative of thought on their topics. What particular encounters with particular authors, case studies, facts, stories, or evidence, during the research process seemed to influence their thinking? Since you've instructed students not to consult their research materials, this writing draws on their recall of what they've read or experienced. Tell them to trust that they'll remember what's important.

- So far, your students have been telling stories, remembering scenes or writing about the details of their research encounters. They will now draw on another literary device: dialogue. Ask them to write an imaginary dialogue about the topic between themselves and someone else, beginning with the most commonly asked question about their topic (for example, "Is it true that AIDS has become a heterosexual disease?" "Is there any evidence that television violence makes people act violently?" and so on). Students need not plan the dialogue. Simply play both roles—questioner and authority—and follow the conversation wherever it goes.

- Finally, ask students to *compose* a response to this question: "So what?" This step encourages them to work out the significance of the topic to their readers, and pushes them towards a tentative statement of their own understandings. What is the most important thing readers should understand about the students' topics? Tell them to work towards a fairly brief statement, perhaps no more than three or four sentences.

Students who have already practiced narrative thinking as note takers will have little difficulty composing a narrative of thought about their research topics, particularly if they are asked to do this exercise after they've gathered enough information on their topics. It is also an exercise that extends the dialectical process, moving students from activities such as fastwriting, which encourages open-ended exploration, to the final step, in which they are asked to compose an assertion that grows from the information they've collected. One of the best outcomes from this writing is that students recover a sense of authority they might have lost as they listened to the chorus of expert voices overwhelm their own. They reassert their control over the material.

I'm pleased if this essaying occurs *during* the research process, even if it results in a more conventional, argumentative, and thesis-driven paper. Students still practice the habits of mind that shape academic inquiry—dialectical thinking, suspending judgment, tolerating ambiguity—and use writing in much the way they have all semester: to think things through. But I want to alert them to possibilities of the research essay as an alternative way to present their material, and perhaps the best way to do that is to share published models.

Features of the Research Essay

If I show my students a piece such as "Why Did God Make Flies?" or an excerpt from Diane Ackerman's *The Natural History of the Senses* or even Ann Hodgman's "No Wonder They Call Me a Bitch," and ask, "What distinguishes this piece from the research you're used to?" I can count on lively responses. "This is nothing like research papers I've written!" they say. "You mean I can write my paper like *this*?" What they immediately see, of course, is how the researched essay can be distinguished from academic writing. That's why a pedagogy that promotes the research essay rather than the formal research paper must acknowledge that, in many instances, what students are attempting is not a usual form of academic writing, but the kind of thinking that sometime produces it. (See Table 4–2, "Features of the Researched Essay".) But what leaves the deepest impression when students read someone like Ackerman on the history of kissing is how engaging, even compelling fact-based writing can be.

> I still remember those summer nights, how my boyfriend would hide in my closet if my parents or brother chanced in, and then kiss me for an hour or so and head back home before dark, and I marvel at his determination and the power of a kiss.

Table 4–2.   Features of the Researched Essay

1. It may incorporate personal experience as evidence.
2. It is frequently written in first person; the writer–researcher is at the center of the discourse.
3. The writer's situation, especially the reasons for his or her interest in the topic, is often explicit.
4. It may use narrative structure as a central organizing principle.
5. The tone is conversational; the writer's voice dominates.
6. It is driven by questions.
7. The thesis may appear later rather than earlier in the text, and the writer's conclusions may be tentative rather than certain.
8. Source material may be more embedded within the writer's own prose than isolated in separate paragraphs or passages.
9. Information may be used not just to support claims, but also to complicate them; sources are not used exclusively as examples but as a means to think something through.
10. It is likely to feature multiple sources of information, including memory or experience, observation, interviews, as well as reading.
11. It represents an "amateur's raid" on the world of specialists. Through familiar anecdote, example, and observation, the researched essay may attempt to exploit the common ground between the topic and the general reader's experience with it.

> A kiss seems the smallest movement of the lips, yet it can capture emotions wild as kindling, or be a contract, or dash a mystery. Some cultures just don't do much kissing. In *The Kiss and Its History*, Dr. Christopher Nyrop refers to Finnish tribes "which bathe together in a state of complete nudity," but regard kissing "as something indecent." Certain African tribes, whose lips are decorated or in other ways deformed don't kiss. But they are unusual. Most people on the planet greet one another face to face; their greeting may take many forms, but it usually includes kissing, nose-kissing, or nose-saluting. There are many theories about how kissing began. Some authorities, as noted, believe it evolved from the act of smelling someone's face, inhaling them out of friendship or love in order to gauge their mood and well-being. (110)

Ackerman merges the autobiographical with the expository; a memory of kissing in the closet becomes the occasion for wondering about the "power of a kiss." Quite naturally, this leads her to consider when kissing first began, a question that leads her momentarily away from herself and towards the historical work of Nyrop and others. Like a good essayist, Ackerman abruptly shifts contexts because it offers her a chance understand her experience differently; and that is her motive for her research, one that is made explicit in her text. Just like Richard Conniff, who wonders what the fly is doing on his beer glass and investigates the answer by reading a 1920s' *Ladies Home Journal* and talking to an entomologist and observing what happens when he attempts to force-feed one of the insects in his kitchen, Ackerman recalls the "earth-stopping, soulful, on-the-ledge of adolescence kissing" (110) of her youth and wonders—as we all might—why it moved her so, and why it still does.

This habit of seeing in the commonplace occasions for wonder also leads the essayist to mine the common ground between writer and reader. We have all seen houseflies land on our glass, and many of us have had kissing adventures in the closet or the back of the Ford. The questions these writers ask are often the ones we might ask ourselves, and they are often posed in the text, then explored, at exactly the moment we might ask them. "Why is it," writes Conniff after exploring the details of the housefly's "appetite for abomination" and its need to fly "erratically" around our kitchens in search of food, that the creature "is . . . so adept at evading us when we swat it?" Why indeed?

> When we launch an ambush as the oblivious fly preens and pukes, its pressure sensors alert it to the speed and direction of the descending hand. Its wraparound eyes are also acutely sensitive to peripheral movement, and they register changes in light about ten times faster than we do. (A movie fools the gullible human eye into seeing continuous motion by showing it a sequence of twenty-four still pictures a second. To fool a fly would take more than two hundred frames a second.) (13–4)

In the final paragraphs of his essay, Conniff finally gets around to addressing the question he posed at the beginning: Why *did* God create flies? After he explains that flies are not inherently disgusting things but instead pick up most of the potentially harmful microbes from "human uncleanliness" onto their bristly bodies, he concludes that the insects exist "to punish human arrogance."

> They mock our notions of personal grooming with visions of lime particles, night soil, and dog leavings. They toy with our delusions of immortality, buzzing in the ear as a memento mori. (Dr. Greenburg assures me that fly maggots can strip a human corpse roughly halfway to the bone in several weeks if the weather is fine). . . . Flies are our fate, and one way or another they will have us.
>
> It is a pretty crummy joke on God's part, of course, but there's no point in getting pouty about it and slipping into unhealthy thoughts about nature. . . . I plan to get a fresh beer and sit back with my feet up and a tightly rolled newspaper nearby. Such are the consolations of the ecological frame of mind. (20)

With passages like this, I will often ask my students how the author orchestrates the use of factual information to keep the prose interesting. They note the effective use of comparisons—for example, the comparison of a fly's ability to detect movement with how the "gullible" human eye is deceived by a movie; the use of strong words, especially verbs—*launch, ambush, flashes, mock, strip, toy*—and the distinctive phrases, like "preens and pukes" or "flies are our fate." They most certainly notice Conniff's presence in such fragments of prose. He is also present as the narrator of his discoveries and through the distinctive register of his voice, as in this memorable sentence: "It is a pretty crummy joke on God's part, of course, but there's no point in getting pouty about it." It is partly the strength of that personality and voice that domesticates the factual information, making it subservient to the writer's purpose. The sources speak *through* Conniff, and always in the service of the story he is telling.

Narrative is the organizing principle of "Why Did God Make Flies?" Conniff not only narrates the story of *what* he found out about flies—and often, it seems, *when* he found it—but provides an account of what he comes to understand about them. As it often does in the personal essays of our students, Conniff's major revelation comes towards the end of his piece, not at the beginning as a conventional thesis statement. While his research essay does have a point, it is not so much an argument as it is merely a logical extension of the story Conniff is telling and the things he has come to know about flies. His thesis is not offered as an assertion free from doubt—an authoritative claim as we normally understand it in academic writing; instead, Conniff presents his main idea casually, as a final thought: "What I am coming around to is St. Augustine's idea that God created flies to punish human arrogance, and not just the calamitous technological arrogance of DDT. Flies are, as one biologist remarked, the resurrection and reincarnation of our own dirt, and this is surely why we smite them down with such ferocity" (20).

All of these things distinguish the research essay from the conventional research paper, but other features do not. For example, there *is* a thesis. Conniff *does* offer specific evidence for the assertions he makes throughout the piece. "Why Did God Make Flies?" is a focused treatment of the topic, driven by "researchable" questions. He uses a range of authoritative sources of information, including interviews with experts, and a range of research methods, from library work to field observations (though he does not use citations).

When I give an essay like Conniff's or Ackerman's to my students, I urge them to pay attention to how the authors crafted their essays to bring facts to life, techniques that they can use in their own essays (Table 4–3). But I also ask them to help me build a list of these similarities and differences to the conventional research paper. It is equally important to talk about how the differences between the rhetorical

Table 4–3.   Bringing Fact-Based Writing to Life: Techniques and Devices

1. **Embed fact in narrative**. Tell the story of the research, or the story of how your ideas about your topic developed as you encountered new information. Look for opportunities to exploit anecdotes, "little" stories that reveal the significance of what you found.

2. **Put people on the page**. Most of the worst fact-based writing creates peopleless landscapes. Give voice to people who are affected by or involved in the topic. Ultimately, what matters most about almost any topic is why it matters to people.

3. **Mine common experience**. What is your typical reader's experience with the topic you're writing about? How can you help him understand that experience in fresh ways?

4. **Let your passion for the topic come through**. It's hard for a reader to care if she doesn't know why you do.

5. **Find a persona and use it**. Adopt a writing voice that makes it obvious from the beginning that you're an individual human being, not a conduit for information.

6. **Answer questions readers might typically ask about the topic**. Do this especially when you think they might ask them.

7. **Cast a wide net**. Don't simply rely on information from reading, but blend material from your own experience and observation and interviews with other people.

8. **Employ surprise**. Like any writing, research-based writing depends on surprise to sustain reader interest. Use surprising information, unexpected methods, apt metaphor, and other revealing comparisons.

9. **Carefully manage the shift from narrative (or anecdote) to exposition**. It is in lengthy exposition that research-based essays tend to drag, especially after a narrative strand. Try to sustain your writing voice throughout the essay and interrupt long expository sections with narrative, anecdote, case study, or dialogue.

10. **Make fact subservient to purpose**. Use information selectively, only if it pushes the piece towards where you want it to go. There is no virtue in simply showing off how much you know.

11. **Fact is just another kind of detail**. Remember how you use sensory detail in personal narrative—to surprise, to inform, to render, but especially to reveal, to "stand in" for a feeling or an idea. Carefully chosen facts can do the same thing. They can say more than they say.

contexts of the magazine article or nonfiction essay and the academic paper differ, and how these differences explain some of the contrasts between them. This should open the ongoing discussion about how the researched essay prepares your students to write papers for other classes.[6] Some connections will be obvious to them. The researched essay teaches useful skills—library and field research methods, note taking, citation, strategies for incorporating sources—but what will be less obvious are those habits of mind I mentioned earlier. In addition to teaching research skills, we are teaching the spirit of inquiry, an understanding about the nature of research that students can draw on whenever they are asked to write a paper that explores a topic outside themselves. At the outset, I share those five habits of mind (see page 106), and remind them of the ways they've already practiced them since the beginning of E 101. I return to these habits of mind again as students complete their research projects, urging them to consider how they may have shaped their experience as researchers. More than anything, I want to reintroduce them to the pleasures of wondering, and kindle their curiosity, a small flame they might carry to other classes and beyond.

Truth and Its Consequences

Students will see the practical benefits of writing research essays, and they may embrace the pleasures of research as discovery, but what will be less obvious to our students is that the research essay can raise questions about the nature of knowledge, questions that they probably have not considered. In my final interview with Carrie, I remember a poignant moment when my persistent questions about the certainty of "facts" seemed to finally jolt her out of subjectivism, at least temporarily. A fact, she said at first, was something "definite," particularly in science: "[I]t's absolutely right, there's no contradicting it, you know. It's not opinion. It's truth." But as I pressed her, she began to waver on that assertion.

Q: Do the Humanities have facts, or is that the exclusive domain of science?

A: I think everything has. Hmmm. I'm not sure on that one. I think everything has facts. Even science, when you're doing chemical reactions, I mean, they're always finding, oh, well, it's definitely this, and then a couple months later—nope, it was this, too. So facts change.

Q: So they're not definite?

A: I don't think they always are. No. I think some things are and some things aren't. I think anyone can try and contradict it. Stuff that's been studied and studied and studied, I guess it could end up being (contradicted) sometimes. I'm contradicting myself.

Q: You're qualifying it. You started out saying facts are things you know are true, and now . . .

A: Now I'm starting to think that all these things that have been challenged, I guess they can be challenged. I guess they aren't always, I don't know. I guess nothing's definite. You take it as being definite. When we read a book, a research book or whatever, I think that we've been all brought up to automatically take it as being the truth, you know.

At the risk of giving into "magical thinking," I would like to think that Carrie's tentative move into multiplicity, and her new-found suspicion of foundational truth came as a direct result of her experience writing the research essay. I don't think that's so, however. Her insights came as much from talk as from writing. As our conversations continued over five weeks, we continually explored the implications of her relativism. Yet I don't think this discussion about her epistemological beliefs would have been nearly as powerful for her without the writing. When we talked about what she meant by an "opinion," for example, it was always anchored to how she was handling her opinions in her essay.

My conversations with Michael and Carrie convinced me that virtually any research pedagogy, but perhaps especially the one I'm proposing here, should feature classroom conversations about ways of knowing. In particular, instructors should help students unpack the meaning of freighted terms like *opinion, fact, truth,* and *idea.* We should present case studies of subjects about which authorities make conflicting and contradictory claims, and ask our students how they might determine "the truth." As students discuss with each other their beliefs about the relationship between, say, an opinion and a fact, instructors should press them to reflect on how those beliefs influence the *practical* decisions they're making as they work on their research essays. For example, how do they assess the worth of another writer's "opinion" as they're reading, and does that determine what they write down in their notebooks? What "facts" have they encountered that conflict? How did they resolve that conflict in their essays? In what forms does "opinion" appear in their drafts, and where does it appear? How does the way they handle quotes in their essays suggest their relationship to authority? What do they see as their larger purpose as researchers— to seek truth, to challenge it, or to simply "express their own opinion," and how does that affect the way they read sources for their papers?

As I interviewed Carrie and Michael, I often saw their beliefs reflected in Perry's stages, or Belenky and co-authors' perspectives, or Charney et. al's constructs. For methodological reasons, I usually withheld these judgements from them during the course of this study. Yet as a matter of classroom practice, I can see no reason why this information about the intellectual development of college students should be withheld from students. While taking great care to avoid suggesting that these studies imply a hierarchy of moral value associated with each stage—in other words, you're a better person if you're a connected knower than if you're a dualist—studies like Perry's and Belenky and colleagues' might help freshman researchers see their own beliefs in context. These works should be used selectively, and presented as contestable claims about the way things are. In this way, they can also provide a useful classroom illustration of how to approach all sources skeptically.

Writing assignments parallel to research essays might be narrative accounts of how students perceive that their ways of knowing have evolved. These might be highly personal accounts of moments that triggered a shift in thinking. For example, students might be asked to explore, through writing, one or more of the following occasions in their lives:

- The first school writing assignment in which you felt your opinions mattered.
- When people made you feel your opinions didn't matter.
- When you stopped believing everything you read in books.
- When you believed that parents or teachers didn't have all the answers. If not them, who did?
- The period of your strongest rebellion against authority.
- When you felt most certain about what was true in life, and when you felt most uncertain about that.
- When you first began to trust your feelings about what's true.
- When and why you got interested in science or humanities, and how that changed the way you see things.

Consistent with what I've argued all along, this approach to helping students reflect on their intellectual development is rooted in the personal. It assumes that changing epistemological beliefs grow out of specific experiences, and also implicate identity. As they tell the story of their intellectual growth, students will see how it continually involved a negotiation between who they were and the roles others presented to them, or as Robert Brooke suggests, their internal understanding of self and their social understanding of who they're expected to be.

In the midst of their research, students are at that moment confronted with a new role—writers who are researching essays. How is that challenging their beliefs about who they are and how they see the world? This discussion should be the starting point for what I believe is a crucial in-class exploration of how this assignment—which departs in many ways from the conventional research paper—reflects a particular epistemology that may be a sharp contrast with their past experiences as academic researchers. This need not be a theoretical discussion at all. Focus again on practical matters: What are the implications of using "I" in a research paper? Is there anything "original" about the way they wrote their essays? Was there anything "objective" about the way they approached their topics? Should personal experience count as evidence? How does revealing their own specific situations change the way they write their essays, and change the way they are read? Do they deal with sources differently when writing a researched essay than they do when writing a term paper?

Getting Personal Without Being Personal

When we give students the freedom to choose research topics that arise from their own experience, they quite naturally resort to the use of first person in their essays. But not all students choose topics with which they have first-hand experience. While Sean, a young student who was determined to explore the causes of the Viet Nam War, certainly couldn't resort to autobiography, he still might have exploited a first-person point of view. Yet he preferred not to. When a student like Sean steps away from the open subjectivity of the essay, does he forfeit the chance to exploit its power to shift his thinking about research and himself as a researcher? It shouldn't. While first person singular and autobiographical thinking are more widely accepted in academic writing, they are hardly the dominant approaches and, in many cases, are simply inappropriate. What might students like Sean learn from the essayist approach I promote here that they might apply to a less openly subjective research essay?

"Being personal, I want to show my students, does not mean being autobiographical," writes Nancy Sommers. "Being academic does not mean being remote, distant, imponderable. Being personal means bringing their judgements and interpretation to bear on what they read and write, learning that they never leave themselves behind even when they write academic essays" (425). This is helpful advice, particularly for students like Sean, who choose research topics that don't easily lend themselves to autobiographical thinking. Yet, in my experience, students find it difficult to imagine any other way to get personal than talking directly about themselves and their own lives.

Gordon Harvey argues that we should help our students understand that presence in the essay can be "both implicit as well as explicit—a matter of felt life in the writing rather than anecdote or self-analysis" (649). He suggests, for example, that "presence is felt, or missed" (650) by a sense of the writer's "motive" for exploring a topic, a sense that is sustained throughout, or by his "control of quotation and detail," particularly if other voices are not allowed to dominate the writing (651–2). Avoiding cliches and stock phrases, and taking care to "find one's own way of saying something," also establish a writer's presence, and so does what Harvey calls "broadenings": those moments in the writing when the essayist leaves textual sources behind and asks larger questions, particularly those that reveal an "experiential grasp of human behavior, of how life tends to go" (652). All of these can register presence, Harvey believes, without using the pronoun *I*.

I'm not sure how many of the "implicitly personal" ways of creating a presence in the research essay will make sense to first-year students. But classroom time should be spent exploring ways to make the research essay personal without necessarily talking directly about one's own experience. Often published essays (or strong student essays) can help. The key is to choose material that uses little or no autobiography, and uses first person singular sparingly. I've found several Lewis Thomas research essays, for example, to be wonderful examples of scientific pieces in which the writer's presence is felt, often without personal anecdote. The following exercise, suggested by a former student, can help your students see how they might register a presence in their essays without necessarily invoking the use of first person or autobiography.

Classroom Exercise:
Finding the Author in the Text

1. Distribute to your class copies of the first ten paragraphs or so of Lewis Thomas' essay "The Music of This Sphere" (1974) or "On Societies as Organisms" (1974); both are in *Lives of the Cell.*

2. Explain that you will read the excerpt from one or both of Thomas' essays aloud, and instruct your students to place an "A" (for author) next to places in the text where they feel Lewis' presence most strongly. These may be moments when students sense the writer's feelings or attitudes towards his subject, or when they get a strong hint of his personality.

3. After you've read the Lewis piece(s) and students have marked it (them), tally each paragraph—how many of your students marked an "A" somewhere in paragraph 1, paragraph 2, and so on?

4. Begin class discussion with those paragraphs that seem to have drawn the most reaction. What are the qualities or characteristics of these paragraphs that account for your students' sense that Lewis registers his presence? Where exactly in the paragraph did they feel that most strongly? Select several additional paragraphs that garnered the most response.

5. As the discussion winds down, ask your students to help you build a list on the blackboard or on newsprint of the ways a writer can make herself felt by a reader *without* resorting to use of autobiography or the first person. What *implicit* ways can a writer reveal her motives, her feelings, her beliefs, and her opinions in a research essay?

Though both of these Lewis Thomas essays are a bit challenging for first-year students, this exercise rarely fails to generate a lively class discussion. When the results are tallied, virtually every paragraph earns an "A," but some passages clearly generate the most response. For example, in Thomas' essay "The Music of This Sphere," a piece that explores how science attempts to record and analyze nature's sounds, the fifth paragraph is always the runaway winner. And it is no surprise. This is the one of the few passages in the essay that shifts to use of first person and personal anecdote. But it is passages like the fourth paragraph in "On Societies as Organisms" that I find fascinating to discuss with students. Here Thomas never talks about himself, but nearly three quarters of the class hears him talking.

> What makes us most uncomfortable is that [ants], and the bees and termites and social wasps, seem to live two kinds of lives: they are individuals, going about a day's business without much evidence of thought for tomorrow, and they are at the same component parts, cellular elements, in the huge, writhing, ruminating organism of the Hill, the nest, the hive. It is because of this aspect, I think, that we most wish for them to be something foreign. We do not like the notion that there can be collective societies with the capacity to behave like organisms. If such things exist, they can have nothing to do with us. (12)

Students immediately notice the powerful and distinctive language here—"huge, writhing, ruminating"; they often comment about how Thomas has found his own way of saying things, comparing ant life to human life in ways the reader may not expect. Insects that go "about the day's business without much evidence of thought for tomorrow" are not the ants or bees we've known, but, thanks to Thomas' wit and clever angle, we see them anew. His interjection of "I think" clearly marks his presence in the text, but less obvious is the way he invokes the "broadenings" that Gordon Harvey discusses. As Thomas ends the paragraph, he muses that "we do not like the notion that there can be collective societies with the capacity to behave like organisms." Then he adds, "If such things exist, they can have nothing to do with us." There are hints from the beginning of this paragraph that the writer is offering a larger, personal view of the significance of insect behavior as a metaphor for human society. Students notice the word *us* in the first sentence, for example, and implicitly sense Thomas' intention of drawing tighter the connection between human and insect life. He then heightens the tension in those final two sentences, implying that connection makes "us" profoundly uncomfortable.

If you encourage students to consider *where* in a paragraph they often placed their "A's," they will likely notice that they come at the beginning of the paragraph, and especially at the end. There the writer is most likely to make his move to surprise, to comment, to suddenly tighten the seams between things. Thomas does this, too, and we feel his presence behind the words, all of which seem to belong distinctly to him.

Thomas also registers his presence—though students rarely pick up on it—later in "On Societies as Organisms" when he uses an extended quotation from an essay in *Nature*. Students will recognize the situation. They've got a great quote from a source, but how do they *control* it, making sure, while they incorporate the words of another, that they stay faithful to their own purposes and persona? Since this is not a passage that students mark very often with an "A," I always bring it up in class.

> The system of communications used in science should provide a neat, workable model for studying mechanisms in human society. Ziman, in a recent *Nature* essay, points out, "the invention of a mechanism for the systematic publication of *fragments* of scientific work may well have been the key event in the history of science." He continues:
>
> A regular journal carries from one research work to another the various . . . observations which are of common interest. . . . A typical scientific paper has never pretended to be more than another little piece in a larger jigsaw—not significant in itself but as an element in a grander scheme. *This technique, of soliciting many modest contributions to the store of human knowledge, has been the secret of Western science since the seventeenth century, for it achieves a corporate, collective power that is far greater than an individual can exert* [italics mine].
>
> With some alternation in terms, some toning down, the passage could describe the building of a termite nest. (15)

How does Thomas demonstrate "control over quotation and detail," which Harvey suggests signals an author's presence? Have an extended discussion with your students about this because the Thomas passage is rich in practical implications about how to use outside sources in a research essay, or any research paper, for that matter.

To begin with, Thomas clearly chooses a quotation that serves his larger purpose of suggesting that the work of science and the work of insects are surprisingly similar. This is not a quotation that is simply "stuck in," but one that pulls together various strands in the essay that Thomas has woven. He use italics to emphasize ideas that are most important to him, and manipulates the quotation with ellipses, eliminating fragments from the original text that are unnecessary. In the opening paragraph, Thomas also *embeds* a passage from the source in his own writing, using it to amplify his initial assertion that the workings of science might be a great analogy for the workings of human society. At the end, however, Thomas makes the more dramatic move that finally captures Ziman's ideas and thrusts them into a new context that the essayist has created: If the workings of science might mimic the workings of society, and both sound an awful lot like the ways termites build a nest, then perhaps insects and humans are more alike than we like to think. It is this *follow-up* of a quoted passage that our students often neglect. But it is there, after another author has spoken, that the writer's presence is most keenly felt.

Students who are used to writing research papers that are argumentative or based on the thesis-example model may see only two moves they might make following a quoted source: signal agreement or disagreement, or offering up the quote as a supporting example. But there are other possibilities, especially for the essay writer. She might circle back to restate—in her own words—the idea that is most important to her, or apply that idea to a fresh context, as Thomas does here. She might pose a question that complicates the author's claims rather than simply register agreement or disagreement. She might simply wonder (in writing) about the possible significance of the idea or the information—how does it change the story she is telling about her topic or the story of her thinking about that topic? Harvey's "control of quotation and detail," therefore, can be more than simply using a source selectively, chosen to serve the writer's purpose. For the essay writer, the words and ideas of others can be used to deliberately disrupt or complicate or extend the writer's thinking. It is this act of "trying out" the possible significances of what she has found that establishes the essayist's presence, often poignantly. And it is possible without ever saying "I."

While the assignment I've proposed asks students to "get personal," that must be conceived of in the broadest possible way. Harvey's notion of "presence" that does not necessarily involve self-reference makes room for students like Carrie, who admits that she liked her research essay much more than the autobiographical essays she wrote for her Freshman English course. Writing "strictly" autobiography was difficult, Carrie told me, "because it's all me." She preferred the research essay, she said, because "it's easier for me to have other people's opinions to put my opinion on. It's kind of hard to give an opinion about myself . . . I'm kind of going with the paper [in this case]. I'm learning as much as I'm writing so it's not that I'm just reciting my life." While I think that autobiographical essays that just "recite a life" are not what we have in mind, Carrie is like a number of students I've had over the years who are uncomfortable with confessional writing. These students often find the research essay a much more comfortable and enlightening project, especially if notions of the personal are broadly conceived.

But most students seize at the opportunity to "think through autobiography," or as Nancy Miller put it, to invite "the chain of associa-
tions that I am pursuing in my reading [to pass] through things that
happened to me" (11). We like watching those undulating lines under
our feet.

Deflating the Balloons

My eighth-grade dance teacher was a slender man, with long side-
burns and thick, wavy auburn hair that obediently stayed in place,
even through "The Jerk." I remember there was a great deal of initial
enthusiasm about dance class among the boys and girls of Elm Place
Junior High. Most thirteen-year-olds are desperate for physical contact, and in an age when teenage promiscuity was still considered bad
form, slow dancing was the closest thing to sex. But Mr. Schommer
had other ideas. He insisted that the girls wear white gloves, minimiz-
ing hand contact, and he forbade close dancing. "You will always
dance as if there is an inflated balloon between you and your partner,"
he said. He then demonstrated with his wife, who usually handled the
45-rpm records. I will never forget the sight of the two of them, whirl-
ing around the gymnasium—he in a double-breasted blue coat and sil-
ver ascot, she in something unmemorable—dancing as if they had a
distinct disliking for each other.

If ice skating offers me a metaphor for essaying, then Mr. Schommer and his wife—and all of us on those Thursday evenings who were
forced to imitate them—are a competing metaphor for the conventional research paper assignment. Urged to be objective, to efface any
direct evidence of their relationship to the material, students dance at
arm's length to their topics, and as the distance grows, so does the dislike for them. Asked to prove, rather than explore, students avoid the
genuine conversation that comes with more intimate contact. Challenged to make original contributions to knowledge, to practice (pretend?) being scholars in the scientific tradition, students watch their
feet in despair, hoping at least to do the right steps. While it is true that
I learned how to do the box step this way, it was never a dance I appropriated with any understanding, or a dance I ever enjoyed.

I've advanced the argument in this book that it's time that we deflate the balloons. As an introduction to research, freshmen should be
encouraged to embrace their topics with wonder, passion, and a strong
desire to find out, rather than to prove. Rather than pretending false
authority, they should acknowledge their subjectivity, and by doing so,
they may discover what Michael did: a kind of objectivity that allows
them to approach sources more openly.

I've proposed here that we shift the emphasis of our research paper pedagogy from the imitation of the traditional products of academic discourse to an initiation in the process of inquiry: how to ask meaningful questions, resist quick judgements about what is true, and participate in an ongoing conversation. I've tried to make the case that if the research assignment engages our students' beliefs, feelings, and experiences, it is much more likely to entangle them in questions of identity, particularly the roles they see for themselves as students, writers, researchers, and knowers.

These questions become even more compelling as students see themselves writing for a real audience, rather than an abstract or narrowly limited one, to whom they genuinely wish to communicate. And as they see their research as part of a rhetorical tradition that encourages a public discourse on matters of general concern, they discover that a commitment to their beliefs involves a social responsibility. By assuming that their audience needs to be convinced that their research matters, students are challenged to put their topics—and their ideas about them—to the pragmatist's test: What difference will they make in people's lives?

I believe the research *essay,* not the traditional freshman research paper, will encourage these things. Simply renaming the assignment will not make much difference, obviously, and even changing some methods of instruction may not result in the kinds of papers and practices we hope for. As I asserted in an earlier chapter, the research paper is a genre captive to its history. It is laden with nineteenth-century assumptions about the nature of academic research, has long been considered the untouchable centerpiece of composition's service obligation to other disciplines, and has been a largely static fixture in composition textbooks for over 60 years.

Few things remind me more of the difficulty of dislodging inherited assumptions about the research paper genre than my work with high school teachers. While dislike of the assignment runs deep among these instructors, I often discover that the pleaders for euthanasia are among the formal research paper's biggest defenders. I'll never forget the indignation of one high school English department head—someone who earlier had bitterly complained about the quality of her students' research papers—after I handed out a copy of a student paper on New England gravestones, a narrative of her search for her ancestors in Cape Cod cemeteries and what it taught her about the symbolism of early American headstones. "This isn't a research paper," he sniffed. "This is—I don't know what this is. But it's too informal, it lacks scholarly detachment, it lacks an introduction with a thesis, a body, a conclusion. What are you people doing over there?"

What are we doing? We're trying to turn Toms into Hucks, teach students to skate backwards on thin ice, and deflate the balloons. I didn't have that answer at the time, of course. Next time, I will.

Notes

1. I'm often asked which "rules" I wouldn't suspend, and particularly whether I insist that students cite sources. While I see value in teaching the informal research essay without citations, I encourage freshmen to learn to use the conventions for two reasons: It *is* a practical skill we can teach to students that is useful in later courses and that doesn't compromise our claim to the essay, and it reinforces the idea that knowledge is socially constructed, or as Montaigne put it, "Opinions are grafted one on another. The first serves as stock for the second, the second for the third" (349).

2. For years I've been using a piece by Richard Conniff, "Why God Created Flies," which appeared in *Audubon Magazine* a few years back and is now included in his collection of nonfiction essays, *Spineless Wonders*. It's not only carefully researched, but funny, and interesting to most students who love the commonplace subject. I've included the piece in both editions of my textbook, *The Curious Researcher*, because students respond to the essay with such enthusiasm.

3. Encouraging classroom discussion of academic essays by personal literary critics like Tompkins, Nancy Sommers, and Miller, as well as those who practice personal scholarship in other disciplines, like Patricia Williams (law), Susan Krieger (sociology), and Naomi Weisstein (biology), can provide students with inspiring examples of this personal scholarship. They also help students locate their own research essays as further experiments in this alternative tradition.

4. My desire to equate "internally persuasive discourse" with voice needs to be qualified. Bahktin's version of voice, as I understand it, assumes that it doesn't "belong" to a writer as some kind of linguistic reflection of the "true" self. Voice, or any words we claim to possess, are always only "half ours" and "half someone else's." Because of this, voice is a dynamic not a static thing, particularly as we appropriate new discourses and attempt to make them our own. A writer doesn't find *a* voice, then, but is continually constructing new voices.

5. This exercise is partly modeled after the "looping" method described in Peter Elbow and Pat Belanoff's text, *A Community of Writers*.

6. The great risk of proposing an unconventional form like the research essay is that students will simply dismiss it as perhaps interesting, but not very useful. I'm mindful of Barbara Walvoord and Lucille McCarthy's study, *Thinking and Writing in College*, which describes students writing papers in four different disciplines. One of their observations, based on interviews with students, was that "students seemed to devalue papers that were not labeled research or term papers" (61).

Appendix A

Three Constructs of Student Epistemologies

Perry's "Stages" of Intellectual Development

Simple dualism —
— Complex dualism —
— — — — — Relativism —

Position 1 and 2	Position 3 and 4	Position 5 and 6	Position 7, 8, and 9
		Commitment in Relativism	
Begins by seeing only right and wrong, good and bad. Authority mediates Truth. Later, sees diversity of opinion, but accounts for it as Authorities mishandling their job as mediators of Truth.	Disagreement and uncertainty is legitimate but temporary because Authorities can't "find the answer yet." Later, "everyone is entitled to their own opinion," a view set against Authorities' insistence on judging. Or belief that we "just have to think the way They want us to." Relativism may be a special case—in some things, there is still "right" or "wrong." Position 4 is most typical of second semester freshmen.	Relativism becomes generally applied method of thought rather than special case. Authority has The answer in some things (physics) but not in others (English). Later, realization that despite relativistic world one must make choices, commitments, take responsibility (for studies, vocation, morality), though there are risks. Reason can help, but it has its limits.	Commitment to commitment. Stronger sense of identity, that acting in an uncertain world requires faith.

Belenky et al.'s Epistemological "Perspectives"

Silence

Women who feel "subject to whims of external authority." Knowledge resides in others. Lacking introspection, "dialogue with the self." Feel both "deaf and dumb."

Received Knowledge

Dualists—see situations as black and white, believe there is single "right" answer. Truth resides in external Authority, to whom they must listen attentively and then regurgitate learned truths. They do not, however, identify with Authority.

Subjective Knowledge

Truth may reside not in external authority but in self; it is personal, private, intuitive. Truth may also be "grounded" in personal experience—their own and others like themselves. Distrust of traditional Authority sometimes becomes distrust of its methods: theory, abstraction, science, logic. Women begin to "hear themselves think," inner voice, but may lack confidence in their public voice.

Procedural Knowledge

Women recognize that they are not being judged on their opinions, but the method of arguing them. Acceptance that perceptions differ, but interest in how they are determined. Two manifestations: "separate" knowers use "impersonal reason" to argue point they may not be personally committed to, "connected" knowers attempt to understand through empathy. Argument vs. conversation.

Constructed Knowledge

Attempt to merge thought and feeling, personal knowledge and external knowledge. The "truth" of an opinion is a function of context. Higher tolerance for ambiguity, complexity, contradiction. Learn to *care* to know—"passionate knowers . . . who establish a communion with what they are trying to understand."

Charney et al.'s Epistemological Constructs

Absolutism

Essentially dualists who believe "truth can be fully determined." Because truth exists outside themselves, they are absolved of any responsibility —"things are just the way they are." The truth can be determined by consulting appropriate authorities or objective perception.

Relativism

Truth cannot be objectively determined because all "sources of knowledge" are equally valid. Conflict is inescapable because everyone has a different version of the truth, depending on his or her specific circumstance or view. Action is based on what "seemed like a good idea at the time," because opinions are always changing.

Evaluatism

Approximate truth can be determined by using appropriate methods and reason, carefully evaluating evidence and discussion with others. Not all opinions have the same validity. Differing perspectives are a function of particular "frameworks" for seeing that can be evaluated and compared. Acceptance of personal responsibility for decisions because their validity can be judged.

Appendix B

Teaching the Double-Entry (or Dialogue) Journal

Ann Berthoff champions the double-entry journal as a wonderful means for helping students see that they can make meaning "from the first." As students respond to a reading assignment, conduct observations, or do research for an essay, the dialogue journal engages them immediately in interpretation, judgement, speculation, restatement, and question asking. The problem with note cards is that they delay this meaning making until later, and turn initial encounters with texts or the world into hunting-and-gathering expeditions. Your students may, at first, embrace the dialogue journal as a refreshing alternative to index cards, but then the resistance may set in. Doing so much writing as they read or observe might seem inefficient, interfering with their determination to simply collect as much stuff as they can on their research topic and deal with it later (usually the night before the draft is due). One way to sell the dialogue journal is to try to convince your students that they are actually writing their drafts *as* they do their research, saving time later on.

Another way to generate more enthusiasm for the method is to avoid being rigid about how your students should approach the journal. Encourage them to fashion their own approach, while making sure they preserve the conversational spirit of the dialogue journal. I describe the following basic method—a technique that uses opposing pages of a notebook, the left side for collecting material from texts or observations and the right for interpreting and exploring their possible significances—but this can be altered in a number of ways. For example, some students prefer what I call the "research log." This is particularly useful for responding to texts and for students who like to write on computers.[1] After reading the source material once, the student fastwrites an open-ended response, exploring one or more of the questions listed in the right column for the double-entry method, which follows. Then the student rereads the piece, taking notes on key ideas through paraphrase or summary, collecting striking quotations or listing important facts. Then the student repeats the fastwrite, perhaps extending his initial response but keeping in mind the particular ideas, facts, and quotations he collected since he first considered the material. A template for a research log like this one can be designed easily on the computer and used repeatedly. The simplest variation on the dialogue journal is to first take notes on the text or in the field and then allow time for reflective writing after the information or observations have been collected. The questions that follow should provide helpful prompts for this, too.

What I like about the double-entry notebook approach is that it seems to continually invite response and dialogue. The visual arrangement on the notebook page of an author's words and ideas arranged next to the writer's response and interpretation of those ideas nicely simulates conversation as an ongoing and equal exchange. The double-entry notebook also encourages narrative thinking as the writer considers, over time, the author's argument or ideas.

While the double-entry journal can work with any notebook, for the research project you might encourage your students to buy one that will fit in their pockets (4 × 6 inch). These are inexpensive enough to be used exclusively for the research assignment and they are more readily available whenever the researcher makes a field observation or finds a relevant article or book. Tell your students that they will be using opposing pages for their writing—on the left page they will jot down quotes, key ideas, fragments of information, specific observations, or paraphrases from their reading or from the field, and on the right page they will think through writing about what they make of what they collected on the left page. This is a conversation conducted across the spiral binding of their notebooks. It is intended to help them consider the significance of what they are reading or observing, speculate about its relevance to their projects, or how it might change their thinking. Sometimes they will simply write to figure out what an author might be saying, and how they feel about it. Their responses and reactions can be open-ended and are often written quickly, without thinking much about what they're going to say before they say it.

Here's a more detailed description of the approach you can use with your students.

Notes from the Source

- On the left page, collect direct quotations, paraphrases, and summaries of key ideas that you cull from your source

- Or collect specific field observations. What exactly are you seeing? What are you hearing?

- Collect material that's relevant to your project, but also write down passages, facts, and claims from the source that you find surprising or puzzling or that generates an emotional response.

- Make sure you write down this material carefully and accurately.

- Include the page number (if it's a published source) to the left of the borrowed material or idea and complete bibliographic information at the top of the page.

Fastwrite Response

- On the right page, think through writing about what strikes you about what you see on the left page. This may be a messy fastwrite, but it will likely be a focused one.

- Whenever the writing stalls, look left and find something else to respond to.

- Some questions to ponder as you're writing might include
  1. What strikes me about this?
  2. What are my first thoughts when I consider this. And then what? And then?
  3. What does this make me think about or remember?
  4. How would I qualify or challenge this author's claim? In what ways do I agree with it?
  5. What else have I read or heard that connects with this?
  6. How do I feel about this?
  7. What seems most convincing? Least convincing?
  8. Does it change my thinking about the topic? How?
  9. What other research possibilities does it suggest?
  10. If this is a field observation: Is what I'm seeing "typical"; does it challenge my assumptions; are there patterns of behavior I'm observing?

Note

1. This approach is described more fully in my textbook for students, *The Curious Researcher.*

Appendix C

The Internet
and Student Research

The single most dramatic change that has occurred in student research since the freshman "source theme" first appeared seventy years ago is use of the Internet. In the past two years alone, I've seen an explosion in the number of online documents cited by my students in their research essays. For a growing minority of my students, the Web is the first place they look for information. What are the implications of widespread Internet use as an information source for student writing? And are the implications different for those of us who encourage the researched essay rather than the conventional research paper?

The Internet and student research create certain problems and opportunities, regardless of pedagogy:

- The appeal of computers and the dynamic nature of the Internet makes research more appealing to many students who otherwise dislike research writing.

- Unfortunately, many students—and computerphiles especially— ignore the value of library research or field observations.

- Because the collections of an increasing number of libraries in the United States and around the world are going online, student researchers have more opportunity to access a greater range of materials.

- However, the disorganization of information on the Internet makes finding material difficult.

- Because of the democratic nature of online publishing—virtually anyone can "publish" on the Internet—it becomes more imperative to evaluate the credibility and reliability of Internet sources, something that is often difficult to do, particularly for student researchers.

- The ease of downloading text from the Internet and importing that material into students' papers, using the cut-and-paste function in word processing programs, make plagiarism more likely. In extreme cases, students can download entire research papers from the growing number of Web sites devoted to providing "model" papers to students in need.

The research paper pedagogy recommended in *Beyond Note Cards* addresses a few of these problems. Teaching the research essay—rather than the conventional research paper—makes the downloading of entire texts from Web sites like SchoolSucks.Com less likely because the writer has a strong presence in the text. The generic, authorless research paper that is typically available at such Web sites simply won't do. The note-taking strategy recommended here is also, I believe, the best antidote to plagiarism of any source, including online texts. If students are encouraged to write in the middle of the research process, they are much less likely to be tempted to dump material from other sources into their own texts, an event that usually occurs in moments of desperation in the waning hours before a deadline. Most of the challenges that Internet use presents apply equally to the research paper and the research essay. Here are some suggestions about what to do about them.

An Approach for Evaluating Online Sources

The usual approaches for establishing the authority of traditional scholarship and publications often don't apply to Internet material. For one thing, many Internet documents are anonymous, and the date of publication isn't always clear. In some cases, even if there is an author of an online document, his or her affiliation or credentials may not be apparent. These shortcomings notwithstanding, our students will turn to the Internet in increasing numbers to find information for their essays. How can we help them evaluate the credibility of online sources? It isn't always easy, but if you ask your students to follow these steps, they are more likely to make better judgements about whether to use something in their essays that they find online.

1. **Does the document have an author or authors? If** *yes,* **go to step 2. If** *no,* **go to step 10.**

2. Does the document appear in an online journal or magazine that is "refereed?" In other words, is there any indication that every article submitted must be reviewed by other scholars in the field before it is accepted for publication? If so, you've found a good source. If not, go to step 3.

3. Is the document from a governmental source? If *yes*, then it may be a good source. If *no*, go to next step.

4. Does the document appear in an online publication affiliated with a reputable educational institution or organization? If not, go to step 5.

5. Is *the author* affiliated with a reputable educational institution or organization? (For example, is he or she connected with a large university or a national nonprofit organization? Individuals associated with businesses or special interest groups may be reliable, though researchers should be vigilant about whether these individuals have axes to grind. If you end up using the information from a commercial or political site, qualify the information to make any biases clear.) If so, be encouraged. If not, move on to the next step.

6. If the author isn't clearly affiliated with a reputable institution, does he or she offer any credentials that help establish his or her expertise to write on the topic? (For example, an advanced degree in the relevant discipline is encouraging.) If *no*, go to step 7.

7. Did you find the document in a Web site that has earned high marks from scholarly reviewers and others interested in the reliability of Internet information? (See "Other Ways to Avoid Disinformation on the Internet" in the section that follows for ways to check this.) Yes? Great. No? Move on.

8. Does the author include an email address link on the online document so that you can write to inquire about affiliations or professional credentials or other publications on the topic? If not, go to the next step.

9. Has the author published elsewhere on the topic in reputable journals or other publications? Check this at the library by searching under the author's name in the electronic catalogue or appropriate CD-ROM indexes. If *no*, reconsider the value of the source. You could be dealing with a lone ranger who has no expertise on your topic and no relevant affiliations.

10. **If the online document has no author, is it from an institutional source like a university, state or federal government, or nonprofit organization? If *yes*, go to step 11.**

11. Is the material from the federal or a state government? If so, that's encouraging. If not, go to step 12.

12. Is the anonymous document published in an online journal or magazine? Is it refereed? (See step 2.) If so, it's likely a good source. If not, go to next step.

13. Is the document part of a publication or Web page from a non-governmental source the mission of which is described in the document, and does it suggest that the organization's goals include research and education? Is there a board of directors, and does it include professionals and academics who are respected in the field? If not, go to the next step.

14. Does the Web site in which the document is located get high marks from scholarly or other reviewers interested in the reliability of Internet information? (See "Other Ways to Avoid Disinformation on the Internet" in the section that follows for ways to check this.) If not, start to wonder whether you should use this source. Go to step 15 before giving up on it.

15. Even if the organization offering the information represents a special interest group or business (for example, the Forest Products Association, or Microsoft Corporation) with an axe to grind, the information may be useful as a means of presenting their point of view. Make sure, if you use it, to qualify the information to make that obvious.

16. Do any of the usual criteria for evaluating a source apply to this anonymous document? Does it have a citations page, and do the citations check out? Was it published on the Internet recently? Does the argument the writer is making seem sound? Do the facts check out? If the answer is *no* to all of these questions, then don't trust the document. If you can answer *yes* to more than one of these questions, the material probably has marginal value in a college paper, though there might be exceptions.

Other Ways to Avoid Disinformation on the Internet

Not surprisingly, scholars, librarians, and others share the concern about the reliability of the Internet for research. To address the problem, a growing number of Web sites—usually sponsored by universities—are devoted to reviewing Internet information and offering researchers links to authoritative online scholarship. The following are just a few of these sites that I've found useful:

Infomine: Scholarly Internet Resource Collections (http://
lib-www.ucr.edu/)
Sponsored by the University of California, this site offers over 9,500
links to Web sites and databases useful to college researchers. The
material is indexed under subject headings such as "Biological,
Agricultural and Medical Sources" and "Social Sciences and the
Humanities." *Infomine* also features a search feature, which allows
the user to look with keywords, as well as subject and title.

Britannica Internet Guide (http://www.ebig.com)
This site is the Encyclopedia Britannica's contribution to sorting the
wheat from the chaff on the Internet. Editors review millions of
Web sites for reliability, including checking the credentials of
authors or organizations, the usefulness of the information, and the
frequency of updates. Currently, only 75,000 sites have passed
muster. But the list includes sites in fourteen categories. The service
is free.

Internet Scout Project (http://wwwscout.cs.wisc.edu/scout/index.html)
Every week, this site publishes the *Scout Report*, which describes
Internet resources that have managed to survive the "highly
selective" review of the librarians and scholars who contribute to
the project. Perhaps the most useful feature is the *Scout Report
Signpost*, a page that allows the user to search three years' worth of
Scout Report–approved sites in a range of fields. What you get is a
summary of the Internet resource and a link to retrieve it.

Making the Most
of an Internet Search

Student researchers aren't particularly methodical under the best of
circumstances; unfortunately, it's a failing that can be deadly when
doing Internet research. Because online resources are so disorganized,
and, unlike the library, there are not currently references that offer
reliable coverage of existing material on a topic, Internet researchers
have to resort multiple searches. Instruction in online searching strategies needs to become a fixture in any research pedagogy, including
this one. I describe more fully elsewhere a step-by-step approach to
teaching students both library and Internet search methods,[1] but a few
tips might be useful here.

First, students need to understand how to define search terms and
the methods of combining them using Boolean connectors. Internet
"search engines" often use the Boolean AND, OR, and NOT, but just as
often they use other connectors or symbols, like quotation marks or

parentheses around a phrase that must appear in a document, or a + or – sign as a substitute for AND or NOT. In recent years, I spend more and more time instructing students in how to choose productive terms for both library and Internet searches. I've come to believe that the words students use to conduct their electronic searches frequently make or break their projects.

Choosing the appropriate search engine for an Internet search is also key. The important thing is never to choose just one, since you can never be sure that it is looking everywhere for relevant documents. That's one reason I encourage students to begin searching by using one of the "metasearch" or "parallel" search engines. These look for Internet resources on a number of search engines at once. For example, *MetaCrawler* (www.metacrawler.com) searches the indexes of nine other search engines (OpenText, Lycos, Webcrawler, Infoseek, Yahoo, TradeWave Galaxy, Excite, Inktomi, and Alta Vista) and returns results from each. *MetaFind* (www.metafind.com) searches using six engines at once. *Mamma* (www.mamma.com) searches seven.

Working with single search engines is still a good idea, even if you use a metasearch. I've found repeatedly that when I do, I turn up even more new material, even if that particular search engine was included in the metasearch. But which should you encourage your students to choose? If students are doing a subject search, *Yahoo* (www.yahoo.com) remains the best. But for a keyword search, which is much more common, *Alta Vista* (www.altavista.digital.com) is probably the best all-around search engine, containing about 100 million entries. But *Northern Light* (www.nlsearch.com), a new search engine, is often particularly appropriate for university research because it organizes the information it retrieves into "search folders" based on subject, type of information, and source, as well as searches approximately one million articles that have appeared in academic journals, books, magazines, and databases. Reprints of the articles cost from $1 to $4.

Internet Resources for Writing Teachers

Bibliography on Evaluating Internet Sources (http://refserver.lib.vt.edu/libinst/critTHINK.HTM)
This is a tremendous site with links to a range of Internet resources that are useful to writing instructors, with the most complete listing of resources on evaluating online material. It also lists print resources on this crucial topic as well.

The Instructor's Guide to Internet Plagiarism (http://rideau.carleton.ca/
~gsenecha/guide/index.html)
This is a useful place to check if you suspect a student is purchasing
a paper on the Internet. It not only has links to the most popular
term paper mills online, but also offers tips about how to determine
whether a paper might be plagiarized from online sources.

Note

1. *The Curious Researcher.* 2nd ed. Boston: Allyn & Bacon, 1998.

Bibliography

Ackerman, Diane. 1990. *The Natural History of the Senses*. New York: Random House.

Adorno, T. W. 1984. "The Essay as Form." Trans. Bob Hullot-Kentor. *New German Critique* Spring–Summer: 151–71.

Anderson, Chris. 1989. "Error, Ambiguity, and the Peripheral: Teaching Lewis Thomas." In *Literary Nonfiction*, ed. Chris Anderson, 315–32. Carbondale: SIUP.

Atkins, Douglas G. 1992. *Estranging the Familiar: Towards a Revitalized Critical Writing*. Athens, GA: University of Georgia Press.

Ballenger, Bruce. 1998. *The Curious Researcher*. 2nd ed. Boston: Allyn & Bacon.

Bahktin, M. M. 1981. *The Dialogic Imagination*. Austin: University of Texas Press.

Baker, Ray P. and William Haller. 1929. *Writing: A First Book for College Students*. New York: Ronald Press.

Baldwin, Charles Sears. 1906. *A College Manual of Rhetoric*. New York: Longmans, Green.

———. 1906. "Freshman English (II)." *Educational Review* 32: 485–99.

Baldwin, Howard Milton. 1930. *A Handbook of Modern Writing*. New York: Macmillan.

Bartholomae, David. 1985. "Inventing the University." In *When A Writer Can't Write*, ed. Mike Rose, 134–65. New York: Guilford.

———. 1995. "Writing with Teachers: A Conversation with Peter Elbow" *College Composition and Communication* 46: 62–71.

Bazerman, Charles. 1987. "Codifying the Social Scientific Style: The APA *Publication Manual* as Behaviorist Rhetoric." In *Rhetoric of the Human Sciences*, eds. John S. Nelson, Allan Megill, and Donald N. McCloskey, 125–44. Madison: University of Wisconsin Press.

———. 1992. *The Informed Writer*. 4th ed. Boston: Houghton.

Belenky, Mary Field, Blythe McVicker Clinchy, Nancy Rule Goldberger, and Jill Matuck Tarule. 1986. *Women's Ways of Knowing: The Development of Self, Voice, and Mind*. New York: BasicBooks.

Bell, Michael Davitt. 1993. *The Problem of American Realism*. Chicago: University of Chicago Press.

Berthoff, Ann E. 1981. *The Making of Meaning: Metaphors, Models, and Maxims for Writing Teachers*. Portsmouth, NH: Boynton/Cook.

Boggs, Arthur W. 1958. "Dear Principal." *English Journal* 57: 86–7.

Boncek, Sandra. Personal Interview. 19 November 1992.

Brent, Doug. 1992. *Reading as Rhetorical Invention: Knowledge, Persuasion, and the Teaching of Research-based Writing*. Urbana, IL: National Council of Teachers of English.

Brereton, John C., ed. 1995. *The Origins of Composition Studies in the American College, 1875–1925*. Pittsburgh: University of Pittsburgh Press.

Brooke, Robert E. 1991. *Writing and Sense of Self: Identity Negotiation in Writing Workshops*. Urbana, IL: National Council of Teachers of English.

Brown, Edwin J. and Maxele Baldwin. 1931. "The Term Paper in College." *Educational Administration and Supervision* 17: 306–13.

Bryan, W. F., Arthur H. Nethercot, and Bernard De Voto. 1931. *The Writer's Handbook*. New York: Macmillan.

Burton, Katherine. 1958. "Some Further Thoughts on Research Papers." *English Journal* 47: 291–92.

Carson, Luella Clay. 1920. *Handbook of English Composition*. New York: World Book Co.

Carter, Kate. Personal Interview. 11 November 1992.

Charney, Davida, John H. Newman, and Mike Palmquist. 1995. "I'm Just No Good At Writing: Epistemological Style and Attitudes Towards Writing." *Written Communication* 12: 298–329.

Chiseri-Strater, Elizabeth and Bonnie Sunstein. 1997. *Fieldworking*. Upper Saddle River, NJ: Prentice Hall.

Conniff, Richard. 1996. *Spineless Wonders: Strange Tales from the Invertebrate World*. New York: Henry Holt.

Connors, Robert J. 1986. "Textbooks and the Evolution of the Discipline." *College Composition and Communication* 37: 178–94.

———. 1988. "Personal Writing Assignments." *College Composition and Communication* 38: 166–83.

———. 1997. *Composition-Rhetoric: Backgrounds, Theory, and Pedaogy*. Pittsburgh: University of Pittsburgh Press.

Cremin, Lawrence A. 1964. *The Transformation of the Schools: Progressivism in American Education, 1876–1957*. New York: Vintage.

Danton, J. Periam. 1963. *Book Selection and Collections: A Comparison of German and American University Libraries*. New York: Columbia University Press.

Davis, Michael. Personal Interview. 31 March 1995.

———. Personal Interview. 7 April 1995.

———. Personal Interview. 19 April 1995.

———. Personal Interview. 28 April 1995.

———. Personal Interview. 5 May 1995.

Dewey, John. 1933. *How We Think*. Lexington, MA: D. C. Heath.

Edmundson, Mark. 1997. "On the Uses of Illiberal Education: As Lite Entertainment for Bored College Students." *Harper's* (September): 34–49.

Elbow, Peter. 1991. "Reflections on Academic Discourse." *College English* 53: 135–55.

Elbow, Peter and Pat Belanoff. 1989. *A Community of Writers*. New York: Random House.

Eldredge, Frances. 1954. "Why 'the' Source Theme?" *College English* 15: 228–32.

Emig, Janet. 1983. *The Web of Meaning: Essays on Writing, Teaching, Learning, and Thinking*. Upper Montclair, NJ: Boynton/Cook, 1983.

Esch, Robert M. 1975. "Research Paper Paranoia." *College Composition and Communication* 26: 42–3.

Fleischaur, W. L. T. 1941–1942. "A Solution for the Teaching of the Investigatory Paper." *College English* 75–8.

Ford, James E. and Dennis Perry. 1982. "Research Paper Instruction in the Undergraduate Writing Program." *College English* 44: 825–31.

Ford, James E., Sharla Rees, and David L. Ward. "Research Paper Instruction: Comprehensive Bibliography of Periodical Sources, 1923–1980." *Bulletin of Bibliography* 39: 84–98.

Friedrich, Hugo. 1991. *Montaigne*. Berkeley: University of California Press.

Frey, Olivia. 1993. "Beyond Literary Darwinism: Women's Voices and Critical Discourse." In *The Intimate Critique*, eds. Diane P. Freedman, Olivia Frey, and Frances Murphy Zauhar, 41–65. Durham: Duke University Press.

Gibaldi, Joseph and Walter S. Achert. 1988. *MLA Handbook for Writers of Research Papers*. 3rd ed. New York: MLA.

Gibbs, Everett W. 1960. "Freshman Research Papers—Once More." *College Composition and Communication* 11: 82–4.

Gilligan, Carol. 1982. *In a Different Voice: Psychological Theory and Women's Development*. Cambridge, MA: Harvard University Press.

Good, Graham. 1988. *The Observing Self*. London: Routledge.

Green, David W. 1986. "Writing, Jargon, and Research." *Written Communication* 3: 364–81.

Greenburg, Robert A. and James G. Hepburn. 1961. *Robert Frost: An Introduction*. New York: Holt Rinehart.

Greenough, Chester Noyes and Frank Wilson Hersey. 1924. *English Composition*. New York: Macmillan.

Greever, Garland and Easly S. Jones. 1939. *The Century Collegiate Handbook*. New York: D. Appleton-Century Co.

Halloran, S. Michael. 1993. "Rhetoric in the American College Curriculum." In *PRE/TEXT: The First Decade*, ed. Victor Vitanza. Pittsburgh: University of Pittsburgh Press.

Hamlin, Arthur T. 1981. *The University Library in the United States*. Philadelphia: University of Pennsylvania Press.

Hart, Michelle. Personal Interview. 5 November 1992.

Harvey, Gordon. 1994. "Presence in the Essay." *College English* 56: 642–54.

Heilker, Paul. 1996. *The Essay: Theory and Pedagogy for an Active Form*. Urbana, IL: National Council of Teachers of English.

Hill, Carrie. Personal Interview. 20 April 1995.

———. Personal Interview. 27 April 1995.

———. Personal Interview. 3 May 1995.

———. Personal Interview. 10 May 1995.

Hodges, John C. 1941. *Harbrace Handbook of English*. New York: Harcourt, Brace.

Hodgman, Ann. 1990. "No Wonder They Call Me a Bitch." *Best American Essays 1990*, ed. Justin Kaplan. New York: Tickner & Fields.

Hook, J. N. and William Ekstrom. 1953. *Guide to Composition*. Chicago: Lippincott.

Hunt, Douglas. 1991. *The Riverside Guide to Writing*. Boston: Houghton.

Hudson, Hoyt H. [1923] 1990. "The Field of Rhetoric." In *Essays on the Rhetoric of the Western World*, eds. Edward P. J. Corbett, James L. Golden, and Goodwin F. Berquist. Dubuque: Kendall/Hunt.

James, William. 1978. *Pragmatism and the Meaning of Truth*. Cambridge: Harvard University Press.

Jehng, Jhin-Chang J., Scott D. Johnson, and Richard C. Anderson. 1993. "Schooling and Students' Epistemological Beliefs About Learning." *Contemporary Educational Psychology* 18: 23–35.

Kauffmann, R. Lane. 1988. "The Skewed Path: Essay as Un-methodical Method." *Diogenes* 143: 66–92.

Kitzhaber, Albert R. 1990. *Rhetoric in American Colleges, 1850–1900*. Dallas: Southern Methodist University Press.

Kotler, Janet. 1989. "Reading for Pleasure: The Research Paper Reconsidered." *Freshman English News* 18.1: 33–7.

Larson, Richard J. 1982. "The 'Research Paper' in the Writing Course: A Nonform of Writing." *College English* 44: 811–16.

———. Personal Interview. 12 October 1992.

Leonard, Arthur Willis and Claude Moore Fuess. 1929. *Practical Precise Writing*. New York: Harcourt.

Lester, James D. 1990. *Writing Research Papers*. 6th ed. Glenview, IL: Scott, Foresman.

Limerick, Patricia Nelson. 1993. "Dancing with Professors: The Trouble with Academic Prose." *New York Times Book Review* 3: 23–4.

Lippold, Timothy. Personal Interview. 19 November 1992.

Lynch, James J. and Bertrand Evans. 1963. *High School English Textbooks: A Critical Examination.* Boston: Atlantic Monthly Press.

Lyons, Nona. 1990. *Making Connections: The Relational Worlds of Adolescent Girls at Emma Willard School.* Cambridge, MA: Harvard University Press.

Macrorie, Kenneth. 1986. *I-Search Paper,* rev. ed. Portsmouth, NH: Boynton/Cook.

Manning, Ambrose N. 1958. "The Present Status of the Research Paper in Freshman English: A National Survey." *College Composition and Communication* 12: 73–8.

Miller, Nancy. 1991. *Getting Personal: Feminist Occasions and Other Autobiographical Acts.* New York: Routledge.

Moffett, James. 1983. *Teaching the Universe of Discourse.* Portsmouth, NH: Boynton/Cook.

Montaigne, Michel de. 1958. *Essays.* Trans. J. M. Cohen. Middlesex, England: Penguin.

Newkirk, Thomas. 1989. *Critical Thinking and Writing: Reclaiming the Essay.* Urbana, IL: National Council of Teachers of English.

Newman, J. H. 1993. "A Structural Investigation of Intellectual Development and Epistemological Style in Young Adults." *Dissertation Abstracts International* 54: 2786B.

Olbricht, Erika. E-mail to author. 12 May 1995.

"Panel and Workshop Reports, CCCC: The Research Paper in Freshman English." 1958. *College Composition and Communication* 9 (October): 178–9.

Pence, R. W. 1944. *The Craft of Writing.* Harrisburg, PA: Stackpole.

Penrose, Ann M. and Cheryl Geisler. 1994. "Reading and Writing Without Authority." *College Composition and Communication* 45: 505–20.

Perry, William. 1970. *Forms of Intellectual and Ethical Development in the College Years.* New York: Holt.

Picard, M. Dane. 1995. "Earthquake News." *Journal of Geological Education* 43: 542–7.

"Reinventing Undergraduate Education: A Blueprint for America's Research Universities." 1997. The Boyer Commission on Educating Undergraduates in the Research University. 5 May 1998. <http://notes.cc.sunysb.edu/Pres/boyer.nsf>

Rivlin, Harry N. 1942. "The Writing of Term Papers." *Journal of Higher Education* 13: 314–20, 342.

Rudolph, Fredrick. 1962. *The American College and University, a History.* New York: Knopf.

Russell, David R. 1991. *Writing in the Academic Disciplines, 1870–1990: A Curricular History.* Carbondale: Southern Illinois University Press.

Sanders, Scott Russell. 1991. "Speaking a Word for Nature." *Secrets of the Universe: Scenes from the Journey Home.* Boston: Beacon Press.

————. 1991. "The Singular First Person." *Secrets of the Universe: Scenes from the Journey Home*. Boston: Beacon Press.

Schommer, Marlene. 1990. "Effects of Beliefs About the Nature of Knowledge on Comprehension." *Journal of Educational Psychology* 82: 498–504.

Schwegler, Robert A. and Linda Shamoon. 1982. "The Aims and Process of the Research Paper." *College English* 44: 817–24.

Shaugnessy, Mina P. 1977. *Errors and Expectations: A Guide for the Teacher of Basic Writing*. New York: Oxford University Press.

Sommers, Nancy. 1993. "I Stand Here Writing." *College English* 55: 420–8.

Spellmeyer, Kurt. 1993. *Common Ground: Dialogue, Understanding, and the Teaching of Composition*. Englewood Cliffs, NJ: Prentice Hall.

————. 1993. "Language, Politics, and Embodiment in the Life-World." *College English* 55: 265–83.

Slater, John R. 1922. *Freshman Rhetoric*. Boston: Heath.

Smith, Alexander. 1953. "On the Writing of Essays." In *Essays: British and American*, ed. Andrew T. Smithberger. Boston: Houghton.

Steel, Eric M. 1950. *Readable Writing*. New York: Macmillan.

Sullivan, Patricia. 1994. "Revising the Myth of the Independent Scholar." *New Directions in Collaborative Teaching, Learning, and Research*, eds. Sally Barr Reagan, Thomas Fox, and David Bleich. Albany, NY: State University of New York Press. 11–29.

Taylor, Thomas E. 1965. "Let's Get Rid of Research Papers." *English Journal* 54: 126–7.

Tetel, Marcel. 1990. *Montaigne*. Boston: Twayne.

Thomas, Lewis. 1974. *The Lives of a Cell: Notes of a Biology Watcher*. New York: Viking Press.

Twain, Mark. 1989. *The Adventures of Huckleberry Finn*. In *The Norton Anthology of American Literature, vol. 2. 3rd ed.*, eds. Nina Baym et al., 27–214. New York: W. W. Norton.

Veysey, Laurence R. 1965. *The Emergence of the American University*. Chicago: University of Chicago Press.

Walvoord, Barbara E. and Lucille P. McCarthy. 1990. *Thinking and Writing in College*. Urbana, IL: National Council of Teachers of English.

Warfel, Harry R., Ernst G. Mathews, and John C. Bushman. 1949. *American College English*. New York: American Book Company.

Williams, Cecil B. and John Ball. 1957. *Writing: A Functional Approach to College Composition*. New York: Ronald Press.

Wilson, Louis R. 1933. "The Service of Libraries in Promoting Scholarship and Research." *The Library Quarterly* 3: 127–45.

Wilson, Matthew. 1995. "Research, Expressivism, and Silence." *Journal of Advanced Composition* 15.2: 241–60.

Zeiger, William. 1985. "The Exploratory Essay: Enfranchising the Spirit of Inquiry in College Composition." *College English* 47: 454–66.

Ziman, J. M. 1969. "Information, Communication, Knowledge." *Nature* 224: 318–24.